Goethe: A Very Short Introduction

VERY SHORT INTRODUCTIONS are for anyone wanting a stimulating and accessible way into a new subject. They are written by experts, and have been translated into more than 45 different languages.

The series began in 1995, and now covers a wide variety of topics in every discipline. The VSI library now contains over 500 volumes—a Very Short Introduction to everything from Psychology and Philosophy of Science to American History and Relativity—and continues to grow in every subject area.

Titles in the series include the following:

ACCOUNTING Christopher Nobes
ADOLESCENCE Peter K. Smith
ADVERTISING Winston Fletcher
AFRICAN AMERICAN RELIGION Eddie S. Glaude Jr
AFRICAN HISTORY John Parker and Richard Rathbone
AFRICAN RELIGIONS Jacob K. Olupona
AGEING Nancy A. Pachana
AGNOSTICISM Robin Le Poidevin
AGRICULTURE Paul Brassley and Richard Soffe
ALEXANDER THE GREAT Hugh Bowden
ALGEBRA Peter M. Higgins
AMERICAN HISTORY Paul S. Boyer
AMERICAN IMMIGRATION David A. Gerber
AMERICAN LEGAL HISTORY G. Edward White
AMERICAN POLITICAL HISTORY Donald Critchlow
AMERICAN POLITICAL PARTIES AND ELECTIONS L. Sandy Maisel
AMERICAN POLITICS Richard M. Valelly
THE AMERICAN PRESIDENCY Charles O. Jones
THE AMERICAN REVOLUTION Robert J. Allison
AMERICAN SLAVERY Heather Andrea Williams
THE AMERICAN WEST Stephen Aron
AMERICAN WOMEN'S HISTORY Susan Ware
ANAESTHESIA Aidan O'Donnell
ANARCHISM Colin Ward
ANCIENT ASSYRIA Karen Radner
ANCIENT EGYPT Ian Shaw
ANCIENT EGYPTIAN ART AND ARCHITECTURE Christina Riggs
ANCIENT GREECE Paul Cartledge
THE ANCIENT NEAR EAST Amanda H. Podany
ANCIENT PHILOSOPHY Julia Annas
ANCIENT WARFARE Harry Sidebottom
ANGELS David Albert Jones
ANGLICANISM Mark Chapman
THE ANGLO-SAXON AGE John Blair
ANIMAL BEHAVIOUR Tristram D. Wyatt
THE ANIMAL KINGDOM Peter Holland
ANIMAL RIGHTS David DeGrazia
THE ANTARCTIC Klaus Dodds
ANTISEMITISM Steven Beller
ANXIETY Daniel Freeman and Jason Freeman
THE APOCRYPHAL GOSPELS Paul Foster
ARCHAEOLOGY Paul Bahn
ARCHITECTURE Andrew Ballantyne
ARISTOCRACY William Doyle
ARISTOTLE Jonathan Barnes
ART HISTORY Dana Arnold
ART THEORY Cynthia Freeland

ASIAN AMERICAN HISTORY Madeline Y. Hsu
ASTROBIOLOGY David C. Catling
ASTROPHYSICS James Binney
ATHEISM Julian Baggini
THE ATMOSPHERE Paul I. Palmer
AUGUSTINE Henry Chadwick
AUSTRALIA Kenneth Morgan
AUTISM Uta Frith
THE AVANT GARDE David Cottington
THE AZTECS Davíd Carrasco
BABYLONIA Trevor Bryce
BACTERIA Sebastian G. B. Amyes
BANKING John Goddard and John O. S. Wilson
BARTHES Jonathan Culler
THE BEATS David Sterritt
BEAUTY Roger Scruton
BEHAVIOURAL ECONOMICS Michelle Baddeley
BESTSELLERS John Sutherland
THE BIBLE John Riches
BIBLICAL ARCHAEOLOGY Eric H. Cline
BIOGRAPHY Hermione Lee
BLACK HOLES Katherine Blundell
BLOOD Chris Cooper
THE BLUES Elijah Wald
THE BODY Chris Shilling
THE BOOK OF MORMON Terryl Givens
BORDERS Alexander C. Diener and Joshua Hagen
THE BRAIN Michael O'Shea
THE BRICS Andrew F. Cooper
THE BRITISH CONSTITUTION Martin Loughlin
THE BRITISH EMPIRE Ashley Jackson
BRITISH POLITICS Anthony Wright
BUDDHA Michael Carrithers
BUDDHISM Damien Keown
BUDDHIST ETHICS Damien Keown
BYZANTIUM Peter Sarris
CALVINISM Jon Balserak
CANCER Nicholas James
CAPITALISM James Fulcher
CATHOLICISM Gerald O'Collins
CAUSATION Stephen Mumford and Rani Lill Anjum
THE CELL Terence Allen and Graham Cowling
THE CELTS Barry Cunliffe
CHAOS Leonard Smith
CHEMISTRY Peter Atkins
CHILD PSYCHOLOGY Usha Goswami
CHILDREN'S LITERATURE Kimberley Reynolds
CHINESE LITERATURE Sabina Knight
CHOICE THEORY Michael Allingham
CHRISTIAN ART Beth Williamson
CHRISTIAN ETHICS D. Stephen Long
CHRISTIANITY Linda Woodhead
CIRCADIAN RHYTHMS Russell Foster and Leon Kreitzman
CITIZENSHIP Richard Bellamy
CIVIL ENGINEERING David Muir Wood
CLASSICAL LITERATURE William Allan
CLASSICAL MYTHOLOGY Helen Morales
CLASSICS Mary Beard and John Henderson
CLAUSEWITZ Michael Howard
CLIMATE Mark Maslin
CLIMATE CHANGE Mark Maslin
CLINICAL PSYCHOLOGY Susan Llewelyn and Katie Aafjes-van Doorn
COGNITIVE NEUROSCIENCE Richard Passingham
THE COLD WAR Robert McMahon
COLONIAL AMERICA Alan Taylor
COLONIAL LATIN AMERICAN LITERATURE Rolena Adorno
COMBINATORICS Robin Wilson
COMEDY Matthew Bevis
COMMUNISM Leslie Holmes
COMPLEXITY John H. Holland
THE COMPUTER Darrel Ince
COMPUTER SCIENCE Subrata Dasgupta
CONFUCIANISM Daniel K. Gardner
THE CONQUISTADORS Matthew Restall and Felipe Fernández-Armesto
CONSCIENCE Paul Strohm
CONSCIOUSNESS Susan Blackmore
CONTEMPORARY ART Julian Stallabrass
CONTEMPORARY FICTION Robert Eaglestone
CONTINENTAL PHILOSOPHY Simon Critchley
COPERNICUS Owen Gingerich
CORAL REEFS Charles Sheppard

CORPORATE SOCIAL RESPONSIBILITY Jeremy Moon
CORRUPTION Leslie Holmes
COSMOLOGY Peter Coles
CRIME FICTION Richard Bradford
CRIMINAL JUSTICE Julian V. Roberts
CRITICAL THEORY Stephen Eric Bronner
THE CRUSADES Christopher Tyerman
CRYPTOGRAPHY Fred Piper and Sean Murphy
CRYSTALLOGRAPHY A. M. Glazer
THE CULTURAL REVOLUTION Richard Curt Kraus
DADA AND SURREALISM David Hopkins
DANTE Peter Hainsworth and David Robey
DARWIN Jonathan Howard
THE DEAD SEA SCROLLS Timothy Lim
DECOLONIZATION Dane Kennedy
DEMOCRACY Bernard Crick
DEPRESSION Jan Scott and Mary Jane Tacchi
DERRIDA Simon Glendinning
DESCARTES Tom Sorell
DESERTS Nick Middleton
DESIGN John Heskett
DEVELOPMENTAL BIOLOGY Lewis Wolpert
THE DEVIL Darren Oldridge
DIASPORA Kevin Kenny
DICTIONARIES Lynda Mugglestone
DINOSAURS David Norman
DIPLOMACY Joseph M. Siracusa
DOCUMENTARY FILM Patricia Aufderheide
DREAMING J. Allan Hobson
DRUGS Les Iversen
DRUIDS Barry Cunliffe
EARLY MUSIC Thomas Forrest Kelly
THE EARTH Martin Redfern
EARTH SYSTEM SCIENCE Tim Lenton
ECONOMICS Partha Dasgupta
EDUCATION Gary Thomas
EGYPTIAN MYTH Geraldine Pinch
EIGHTEENTH-CENTURY BRITAIN Paul Langford
THE ELEMENTS Philip Ball
EMOTION Dylan Evans
EMPIRE Stephen Howe
ENGELS Terrell Carver
ENGINEERING David Blockley
ENGLISH LITERATURE Jonathan Bate
THE ENLIGHTENMENT John Robertson
ENTREPRENEURSHIP Paul Westhead and Mike Wright
ENVIRONMENTAL ECONOMICS Stephen Smith
ENVIRONMENTAL POLITICS Andrew Dobson
EPICUREANISM Catherine Wilson
EPIDEMIOLOGY Rodolfo Saracci
ETHICS Simon Blackburn
ETHNOMUSICOLOGY Timothy Rice
THE ETRUSCANS Christopher Smith
EUGENICS Philippa Levine
THE EUROPEAN UNION John Pinder and Simon Usherwood
EVOLUTION Brian and Deborah Charlesworth
EXISTENTIALISM Thomas Flynn
EXPLORATION Stewart A. Weaver
THE EYE Michael Land
FAMILY LAW Jonathan Herring
FASCISM Kevin Passmore
FASHION Rebecca Arnold
FEMINISM Margaret Walters
FILM Michael Wood
FILM MUSIC Kathryn Kalinak
THE FIRST WORLD WAR Michael Howard
FOLK MUSIC Mark Slobin
FOOD John Krebs
FORENSIC PSYCHOLOGY David Canter
FORENSIC SCIENCE Jim Fraser
FORESTS Jaboury Ghazoul
FOSSILS Keith Thomson
FOUCAULT Gary Gutting
THE FOUNDING FATHERS R. B. Bernstein
FRACTALS Kenneth Falconer
FREE SPEECH Nigel Warburton
FREE WILL Thomas Pink
FRENCH LITERATURE John D. Lyons
THE FRENCH REVOLUTION William Doyle
FREUD Anthony Storr
FUNDAMENTALISM Malise Ruthven

FUNGI Nicholas P. Money
THE FUTURE Jennifer M. Gidley
GALAXIES John Gribbin
GALILEO Stillman Drake
GAME THEORY Ken Binmore
GANDHI Bhikhu Parekh
GENES Jonathan Slack
GENIUS Andrew Robinson
GEOGRAPHY John Matthews and David Herbert
GEOPOLITICS Klaus Dodds
GERMAN LITERATURE Nicholas Boyle
GERMAN PHILOSOPHY Andrew Bowie
GLOBAL CATASTROPHES Bill McGuire
GLOBAL ECONOMIC HISTORY Robert C. Allen
GLOBALIZATION Manfred Steger
GOD John Bowker
GOETHE Ritchie Robertson
THE GOTHIC Nick Groom
GOVERNANCE Mark Bevir
GRAVITY Timothy Clifton
THE GREAT DEPRESSION AND THE NEW DEAL Eric Rauchway
HABERMAS James Gordon Finlayson
THE HABSBURG EMPIRE Martyn Rady
HAPPINESS Daniel M. Haybron
THE HARLEM RENAISSANCE Cheryl A. Wall
THE HEBREW BIBLE AS LITERATURE Tod Linafelt
HEGEL Peter Singer
HEIDEGGER Michael Inwood
HERMENEUTICS Jens Zimmermann
HERODOTUS Jennifer T. Roberts
HIEROGLYPHS Penelope Wilson
HINDUISM Kim Knott
HISTORY John H. Arnold
THE HISTORY OF ASTRONOMY Michael Hoskin
THE HISTORY OF CHEMISTRY William H. Brock
THE HISTORY OF LIFE Michael Benton
THE HISTORY OF MATHEMATICS Jacqueline Stedall
THE HISTORY OF MEDICINE William Bynum
THE HISTORY OF TIME Leofranc Holford-Strevens
HIV AND AIDS Alan Whiteside
HOBBES Richard Tuck
HOLLYWOOD Peter Decherney
HOME Michael Allen Fox
HORMONES Martin Luck
HUMAN ANATOMY Leslie Klenerman
HUMAN EVOLUTION Bernard Wood
HUMAN RIGHTS Andrew Clapham
HUMANISM Stephen Law
HUME A. J. Ayer
HUMOUR Noël Carroll
THE ICE AGE Jamie Woodward
IDEOLOGY Michael Freeden
INDIAN CINEMA Ashish Rajadhyaksha
INDIAN PHILOSOPHY Sue Hamilton
THE INDUSTRIAL REVOLUTION Robert C. Allen
INFECTIOUS DISEASE Marta L. Wayne and Benjamin M. Bolker
INFINITY Ian Stewart
INFORMATION Luciano Floridi
INNOVATION Mark Dodgson and David Gann
INTELLIGENCE Ian J. Deary
INTELLECTUAL PROPERTY Siva Vaidhyanathan
INTERNATIONAL LAW Vaughan Lowe
INTERNATIONAL MIGRATION Khalid Koser
INTERNATIONAL RELATIONS Paul Wilkinson
INTERNATIONAL SECURITY Christopher S. Browning
IRAN Ali M. Ansari
ISLAM Malise Ruthven
ISLAMIC HISTORY Adam Silverstein
ISOTOPES Rob Ellam
ITALIAN LITERATURE Peter Hainsworth and David Robey
JESUS Richard Bauckham
JOURNALISM Ian Hargreaves
JUDAISM Norman Solomon
JUNG Anthony Stevens
KABBALAH Joseph Dan
KAFKA Ritchie Robertson
KANT Roger Scruton
KEYNES Robert Skidelsky
KIERKEGAARD Patrick Gardiner
KNOWLEDGE Jennifer Nagel

THE KORAN Michael Cook
LANDSCAPE ARCHITECTURE
Ian H. Thompson
LANDSCAPES AND GEOMORPHOLOGY
Andrew Goudie and Heather Viles
LANGUAGES Stephen R. Anderson
LATE ANTIQUITY Gillian Clark
LAW Raymond Wacks
THE LAWS OF THERMODYNAMICS
Peter Atkins
LEADERSHIP Keith Grint
LEARNING Mark Haselgrove
LEIBNIZ Maria Rosa Antognazza
LIBERALISM Michael Freeden
LIGHT Ian Walmsley
LINCOLN Allen C. Guelzo
LINGUISTICS Peter Matthews
LITERARY THEORY Jonathan Culler
LOCKE John Dunn
LOGIC Graham Priest
LOVE Ronald de Sousa
MACHIAVELLI Quentin Skinner
MADNESS Andrew Scull
MAGIC Owen Davies
MAGNA CARTA Nicholas Vincent
MAGNETISM Stephen Blundell
MALTHUS Donald Winch
MANAGEMENT John Hendry
MAO Delia Davin
MARINE BIOLOGY Philip V. Mladenov
THE MARQUIS DE SADE John Phillips
MARTIN LUTHER Scott H. Hendrix
MARTYRDOM Jolyon Mitchell
MARX Peter Singer
MATERIALS Christopher Hall
MATHEMATICS Timothy Gowers
THE MEANING OF LIFE
Terry Eagleton
MEASUREMENT David Hand
MEDICAL ETHICS Tony Hope
MEDICAL LAW Charles Foster
MEDIEVAL BRITAIN John Gillingham and Ralph A. Griffiths
MEDIEVAL LITERATURE
Elaine Treharne
MEDIEVAL PHILOSOPHY
John Marenbon
MEMORY Jonathan K. Foster
METAPHYSICS Stephen Mumford
THE MEXICAN REVOLUTION
Alan Knight
MICHAEL FARADAY Frank A. J. L. James
MICROBIOLOGY Nicholas P. Money
MICROECONOMICS Avinash Dixit
MICROSCOPY Terence Allen
THE MIDDLE AGES Miri Rubin
MILITARY JUSTICE Eugene R. Fidell
MINERALS David Vaughan
MODERN ART David Cottington
MODERN CHINA Rana Mitter
MODERN DRAMA
Kirsten E. Shepherd-Barr
MODERN FRANCE Vanessa R. Schwartz
MODERN IRELAND Senia Pašeta
MODERN ITALY Anna Cento Bull
MODERN JAPAN
Christopher Goto-Jones
MODERN LATIN AMERICAN LITERATURE
Roberto González Echevarría
MODERN WAR Richard English
MODERNISM Christopher Butler
MOLECULAR BIOLOGY Aysha Divan and Janice A. Royds
MOLECULES Philip Ball
THE MONGOLS Morris Rossabi
MOONS David A. Rothery
MORMONISM
Richard Lyman Bushman
MOUNTAINS Martin F. Price
MUHAMMAD Jonathan A. C. Brown
MULTICULTURALISM Ali Rattansi
MUSIC Nicholas Cook
MYTH Robert A. Segal
THE NAPOLEONIC WARS
Mike Rapport
NATIONALISM Steven Grosby
NAVIGATION Jim Bennett
NELSON MANDELA Elleke Boehmer
NEOLIBERALISM Manfred Steger and Ravi Roy
NETWORKS Guido Caldarelli and Michele Catanzaro
THE NEW TESTAMENT
Luke Timothy Johnson
THE NEW TESTAMENT AS LITERATURE Kyle Keefer
NEWTON Robert Iliffe
NIETZSCHE Michael Tanner

NINETEENTH-CENTURY BRITAIN Christopher Harvie and H. C. G. Matthew
THE NORMAN CONQUEST George Garnett
NORTH AMERICAN INDIANS Theda Perdue and Michael D. Green
NORTHERN IRELAND Marc Mulholland
NOTHING Frank Close
NUCLEAR PHYSICS Frank Close
NUCLEAR POWER Maxwell Irvine
NUCLEAR WEAPONS Joseph M. Siracusa
NUMBERS Peter M. Higgins
NUTRITION David A. Bender
OBJECTIVITY Stephen Gaukroger
THE OLD TESTAMENT Michael D. Coogan
THE ORCHESTRA D. Kern Holoman
ORGANIC CHEMISTRY Graham Patrick
ORGANIZATIONS Mary Jo Hatch
PAGANISM Owen Davies
THE PALESTINIAN-ISRAELI CONFLICT Martin Bunton
PANDEMICS Christian W. McMillen
PARTICLE PHYSICS Frank Close
PAUL E. P. Sanders
PEACE Oliver P. Richmond
PENTECOSTALISM William K. Kay
THE PERIODIC TABLE Eric R. Scerri
PHILOSOPHY Edward Craig
PHILOSOPHY IN THE ISLAMIC WORLD Peter Adamson
PHILOSOPHY OF LAW Raymond Wacks
PHILOSOPHY OF SCIENCE Samir Okasha
PHOTOGRAPHY Steve Edwards
PHYSICAL CHEMISTRY Peter Atkins
PILGRIMAGE Ian Reader
PLAGUE Paul Slack
PLANETS David A. Rothery
PLANTS Timothy Walker
PLATE TECTONICS Peter Molnar
PLATO Julia Annas
POLITICAL PHILOSOPHY David Miller
POLITICS Kenneth Minogue
POPULISM Cas Mudde and Cristóbal Rovira Kaltwasser
POSTCOLONIALISM Robert Young
POSTMODERNISM Christopher Butler
POSTSTRUCTURALISM Catherine Belsey
PREHISTORY Chris Gosden
PRESOCRATIC PHILOSOPHY Catherine Osborne
PRIVACY Raymond Wacks
PROBABILITY John Haigh
PROGRESSIVISM Walter Nugent
PROTESTANTISM Mark A. Noll
PSYCHIATRY Tom Burns
PSYCHOANALYSIS Daniel Pick
PSYCHOLOGY Gillian Butler and Freda McManus
PSYCHOTHERAPY Tom Burns and Eva Burns-Lundgren
PUBLIC ADMINISTRATION Stella Z. Theodoulou and Ravi K. Roy
PUBLIC HEALTH Virginia Berridge
PURITANISM Francis J. Bremer
THE QUAKERS Pink Dandelion
QUANTUM THEORY John Polkinghorne
RACISM Ali Rattansi
RADIOACTIVITY Claudio Tuniz
RASTAFARI Ennis B. Edmonds
THE REAGAN REVOLUTION Gil Troy
REALITY Jan Westerhoff
THE REFORMATION Peter Marshall
RELATIVITY Russell Stannard
RELIGION IN AMERICA Timothy Beal
THE RENAISSANCE Jerry Brotton
RENAISSANCE ART Geraldine A. Johnson
REVOLUTIONS Jack A. Goldstone
RHETORIC Richard Toye
RISK Baruch Fischhoff and John Kadvany
RITUAL Barry Stephenson
RIVERS Nick Middleton
ROBOTICS Alan Winfield
ROCKS Jan Zalasiewicz
ROMAN BRITAIN Peter Salway
THE ROMAN EMPIRE Christopher Kelly
THE ROMAN REPUBLIC David M. Gwynn
ROMANTICISM Michael Ferber

ROUSSEAU Robert Wokler
RUSSELL A. C. Grayling
RUSSIAN HISTORY Geoffrey Hosking
RUSSIAN LITERATURE Catriona Kelly
THE RUSSIAN REVOLUTION S. A. Smith
SAVANNAS Peter A. Furley
SCHIZOPHRENIA Chris Frith and Eve Johnstone
SCHOPENHAUER Christopher Janaway
SCIENCE AND RELIGION Thomas Dixon
SCIENCE FICTION David Seed
THE SCIENTIFIC REVOLUTION Lawrence M. Principe
SCOTLAND Rab Houston
SEXUALITY Véronique Mottier
SHAKESPEARE'S COMEDIES Bart van Es
SIKHISM Eleanor Nesbitt
THE SILK ROAD James A. Millward
SLANG Jonathon Green
SLEEP Steven W. Lockley and Russell G. Foster
SOCIAL AND CULTURAL ANTHROPOLOGY John Monaghan and Peter Just
SOCIAL PSYCHOLOGY Richard J. Crisp
SOCIAL WORK Sally Holland and Jonathan Scourfield
SOCIALISM Michael Newman
SOCIOLINGUISTICS John Edwards
SOCIOLOGY Steve Bruce
SOCRATES C. C. W. Taylor
SOUND Mike Goldsmith
THE SOVIET UNION Stephen Lovell
THE SPANISH CIVIL WAR Helen Graham
SPANISH LITERATURE Jo Labanyi
SPINOZA Roger Scruton
SPIRITUALITY Philip Sheldrake
SPORT Mike Cronin
STARS Andrew King
STATISTICS David J. Hand
STEM CELLS Jonathan Slack
STRUCTURAL ENGINEERING David Blockley
STUART BRITAIN John Morrill
SUPERCONDUCTIVITY Stephen Blundell
SYMMETRY Ian Stewart
TAXATION Stephen Smith
TEETH Peter S. Ungar
TELESCOPES Geoff Cottrell
TERRORISM Charles Townshend
THEATRE Marvin Carlson
THEOLOGY David F. Ford
THOMAS AQUINAS Fergus Kerr
THOUGHT Tim Bayne
TIBETAN BUDDHISM Matthew T. Kapstein
TOCQUEVILLE Harvey C. Mansfield
TRAGEDY Adrian Poole
TRANSLATION Matthew Reynolds
THE TROJAN WAR Eric H. Cline
TRUST Katherine Hawley
THE TUDORS John Guy
TWENTIETH-CENTURY BRITAIN Kenneth O. Morgan
THE UNITED NATIONS Jussi M. Hanhimäki
THE U.S. CONGRESS Donald A. Ritchie
THE U.S. SUPREME COURT Linda Greenhouse
UTOPIANISM Lyman Tower Sargent
THE VIKINGS Julian Richards
VIRUSES Dorothy H. Crawford
VOLTAIRE Nicholas Cronk
WAR AND TECHNOLOGY Alex Roland
WATER John Finney
WEATHER Storm Dunlop
THE WELFARE STATE David Garland
WILLIAM SHAKESPEARE Stanley Wells
WITCHCRAFT Malcolm Gaskill
WITTGENSTEIN A. C. Grayling
WORK Stephen Fineman
WORLD MUSIC Philip Bohlman
THE WORLD TRADE ORGANIZATION Amrita Narlikar
WORLD WAR II Gerhard L. Weinberg
WRITING AND SCRIPT Andrew Robinson
ZIONISM Michael Stanislawski

Ritchie Robertson

GOETHE

A Very Short Introduction

OXFORD
UNIVERSITY PRESS

OXFORD
UNIVERSITY PRESS

Great Clarendon Street, Oxford, OX2 6DP,
United Kingdom

Oxford University Press is a department of the University of Oxford.
It furthers the University's objective of excellence in research, scholarship,
and education by publishing worldwide. Oxford is a registered trade mark of
Oxford University Press in the UK and in certain other countries

First edition published in 2016

Published in the United States of America by Oxford University Press
198 Madison Avenue, New York, NY 10016, United States of America

British Library Cataloguing in Publication Data
Data available

Library of Congress Control Number: 2015947579

ISBN 978–0–19–968925–5

Printed and bound by
CPI Group (UK) Ltd, Croydon, CR0 4YY

Contents

Preface

In 1878 the Victorian critic Matthew Arnold wrote: 'Goethe is the greatest poet of modern times, not because he is one of the half-dozen human beings who in the history of our race have shown the most signal gift for poetry, but because having a very considerable gift for poetry, he was at the same time, in the width, depth, and richness of his criticism of life, by far our greatest modern man.'

If we disregard some dated language ('race', 'man'), Arnold has stated the key reasons why Goethe demands our attention. First, Goethe was a great writer. By 'poetry' Arnold means not only lyric poetry, in which Goethe certainly excelled, but literary writing in general. Goethe produced masterpieces in almost every genre: poems on the largest and smallest scale, plays and novels in varied kinds, autobiography, aphorisms, essays, literary and art criticism. Second, Goethe addressed the greatest issues of his—and our—time, and he did so on the basis of unusually wide experience. In private life, he experienced love, marriage, parenthood, friendship, bereavement; in public life, he helped to govern a country (admittedly a very small one) and saw at first hand the horrors of war—a battle, a chaotic retreat, and later the insolence of occupying troops. He never considered becoming a professional writer; for a long time his ambitions were set on visual art, and throughout his life he probably devoted as much time to the study of the natural world as he did to writing.

Goethe claims our attention primarily as a supreme writer, with an exceptional amount of interesting material to write about. I stress this because the image persists of Goethe as a distant and, nowadays, unexciting Victorian sage, and also as a serene Olympian figure above ordinary human passions. Nothing could be more false: Goethe assumed a calm pose precisely in order to control his turbulent emotional experience; and his approach to life was wholly individual. Both in action and thought, he defied convention. He scandalized contemporaries by living for many years in a loving relationship with a woman he was not married to; and on every issue, as Arnold rightly says, Goethe asks implicitly: 'But *is* it so? Is it so for *me*?'. However, though Goethe's essays and aphorisms are rewarding, his main works are literature, and they offer the complexity, the clash of different perspectives, the contradictions, and the avoidance of easy answers, that are characteristic of great literature.

Goethe's works inevitably bear the stamp of the world he lived in. In his youth, we find him chafing against the petty restrictions of the old régime in Germany; in his extreme old age, we find him considering the gains and losses of modernization, and imagining projects of social reform and technical progress. He was deeply marked by living through the French Revolution and the twenty-plus years of war that followed it. Intellectually, he was shaped by the Enlightenment, and by its commitment to understanding the world by means of empirical and historical study, though he rejected the egalitarianism and irreligion of the Enlightenment's radical wing.

In Germany, Goethe has long been an iconic figure. Criticism of him sometimes arouses fury. This has not always been the case. In his lifetime, his opposition to trends such as Romanticism and

German nationalism, and the frequent difficulty of his later works, made him seem marginal. His supposedly immoral domestic life, his detachment from Christianity, his political conservatism, and his employment at a princely court, provoked many attacks. 'Since I began to feel, I have hated Goethe', wrote the left-wing radical Ludwig Börne in 1830; 'since I began to think, I have known why.' It was the official intellectuals of the German Empire, founded in 1871, who elevated Goethe into a cult figure and artificially smoothed his image.

The present book is not a hagiography, nor an attempt at debunking. It is a personal book, in which, without forcing my presence on the reader, I have tried to express my own views about why Goethe matters and why his main works remain endlessly rewarding. I do not offer him as a universal genius or an infallible sage: his achievement in science seems questionable, and his political views have only limited value for the present day. Nevertheless, he was more than just an author: his literary works are intimately connected with his autobiographical and scientific writings, his letters and his many recorded conversations; to explore his immense oeuvre (40 stout volumes, including commentary, in the latest edition) is like exploring a world. This book is intended to help readers into that world.

In quoting Goethe's poems, I have mostly given unambitious literal prose translations, but there are a few instances where no translation can suggest the dignified movement, or the extreme concision, of the original, and in these cases I have reproduced Goethe's German along with a prose translation.

I am very grateful to Matthew Bell, Kevin Hilliard, and Katharine Nicholas for reading the whole of this book in draft, and to Barry Nisbet and Jim Reed for reading parts of it. Their comments have been invaluable. The opinions expressed here are my own, as are any surviving mistakes.

List of illustrations

1. Johann Wolfgang von Goethe, 1811.

Chapter 1
Love

The Sufferings of Young Werther

Goethe is perhaps the greatest love poet of modern Europe, and much of this chapter will be concerned with his poetry. However, it was in his early novel, *Die Leiden des jungen Werthers* (*The Sufferings of Young Werther*, 1774), that he wrote about love in a new way which enraptured innumerable readers. The 25-year-old Goethe, working reluctantly and rather aimlessly as a barrister in his native Frankfurt am Main (see Figure 2), suddenly found himself famous.

The novel, following a favourite 18th-century device, is presented by a fictitious editor who claims to have collected documents with which to recount Werther's life and the circumstances of his suicide. These documents are letters, all written by Werther to a male friend. They bring us so close to Werther's experience that many readers have identified whole-heartedly with him, despite warning signals. Werther comes across as passionate, warm-hearted, responding rapturously to nature. His imagination enables him to project himself into other people's emotions. He is free from snobbery, friendly to ordinary people, loves playing with children, and is repeatedly irked by the social conventions that would restrain his natural impulses. There are, however, ominous hints about his emotional volatility and his past tendency to depression. Nature

2. Goethe's family home in Frankfurt (restored after bombing in the Second World War).

is not enough: he wants love. 'What is the world like without love?' he asks his correspondent. 'Like a magic lantern without a light' (letter of 18 July 1771).

Love is soon embodied in Charlotte (always called Lotte), a young woman in her late teens, who supports her widowed father by looking after her six younger siblings (see Figure 3). She is charming, practical, selfless, but thoroughly corporeal: she and Werther meet at a ball where Lotte admits her fondness for waltzing (a dance then considered rather bold because it involved

3. Werther's first meeting with Lotte, imagined by a 19th-century artist.

physical contact). Werther is soon enraptured. Their relationship is anchored in everyday events that are described simply and freshly, e.g.: 'It is a splendid summer. Often I sit in the fruit trees in Lotte's orchard and with a long pole detach the pears and reach them down from the very tops. She stands below, I lower them to her and she takes them' (letter of 28 August 1771). But even Werther's most vivid images are ominous: the magic lantern implies illusion, the pears suggest forbidden fruit. For Lotte is engaged to Albert, a practical, unimaginative, hard-working administrator, the antithesis of Werther who is a dilettante artist. After Albert's arrival, Werther's frustration makes him as intensely miserable as he was previously ecstatic. His love becomes a tormenting passion; nature now seems a scene of constant destruction; threatened with emotional paralysis, he wanders about at night, forcing his way painfully through thorn-bushes in order at least to feel *something*. Separation from Lotte does not help. Werther takes a job as secretary to an ambassador at a small princely court, but his disregard for social convention gets him into trouble; he resigns his job and is eventually drawn back to live near Lotte, who is now married to Albert.

Here the editor intervenes with a commentary that henceforth alternates with extracts from Werther's letters. We learn that Werther's constant visits are disrupting Albert and Lotte's marriage, and that Werther himself is falling into hopeless depression and has already resolved on suicide. As a prelude, he pays two fateful visits to Lotte. When she remonstrates with him for his self-destructive behaviour, he indicates his inner violence by scowling, grinding his teeth, and accusing her of being Albert's mouthpiece. Later, seemingly calmer, he reads aloud to her from 'Ossian', the elegiac prose-poems by James Macpherson which 18th-century Europe took for an ancient Celtic epic; the intense melancholy overwhelms them, and they meet in a passionate embrace. Lotte regains her self-control and dismisses Werther for good, despite his pleas. Returning home, he arranges his affairs and writes Lotte a long suicide note, interrupting it only to send his servant to Albert to borrow some pistols, on the pretext that he is going on a journey (and therefore needs defence against highwaymen). Lotte guesses why he wants the pistols, but says nothing. Werther shoots himself at midnight and is found, dying, early the following morning.

This was the novel that took Europe by storm and made Goethe a celebrity. 'I know the book almost by heart,' wrote a noblewoman soon after its publication. 'The first part in particular has quite divine passages, and the second is horribly beautiful.' Napoleon, who talked with Goethe for an hour in 1808, had read it seven times. The monster in Mary Shelley's *Frankenstein* (1818) reads *Werther* and finds in it 'a never-ending source of speculation and astonishment', considering Werther himself 'a more divine being than I had ever beheld or imagined'. A French translation appeared in 1776, an English one in 1779. Today the 'Lottehaus' museum at Wetzlar, near Frankfurt, displays not only numerous editions, literary imitations and parodies, but much *Werther*-inspired merchandise, including plates painted in China and showing scenes from the novel or merely suggested by it (Lotte mourning at Werther's grave was a favourite). Why this vogue?

Intensely emotional novels in letters were not new. The 18th century was the age of sentiment as well as the age of reason. Two of its fictional masterpieces, Samuel Richardson's *Clarissa* (1748) and Jean-Jacques Rousseau's *Julie ou la Nouvelle Héloïse* (1761), both based on misguided passion, excited comparable enthusiasm. But while these consist of letters exchanged among several protagonists, in *Werther* all the letters are by the title character, giving the novel unprecedented concentration and intensity. Moreover, Werther's experiences are firmly grounded in a familiar German small-town setting with many homely everyday details. Most importantly, the novel presents love as simultaneously an emotional and a physical experience. 'Oh how it courses all through my veins when by accident my finger touches hers or when our feet touch under the table. I pull back as though from fire and a mysterious force draws me on again—there is a fainting in all my senses', reports Werther (letter of 16 July 1771). And not long before his death he is shocked by experiencing a highly physical erotic dream (letter of 14 December). Goethe went further than any previous writer in presenting his hero as a union of mind and body. In doing so, he extended the range of experience that literature could express. And since literature is not just a commentary on life, but interacts with it, he also extended the range of what people could experience in their lives.

The union of physical and mental experienced in *Werther* corresponds to a major theme in the philosophy, psychology, and medicine of Goethe's time. The late Enlightenment was no longer satisfied with the conception of the mind and body put forward in the 17th century by Descartes. For Descartes, the two were so separate that the body could be imagined as a self-contained machine, though its connection with the mind remained inexplicable. Goethe, like the philosophical doctors of his time, uses the term 'Kraft' ('power' or 'energy') to mediate between physical and mental experience and to link the individual to the natural forces at work around him. Werther uses this word continually, as when he complains 'how narrowly the active and enquiring powers of a human being are confined' (letter of 22 May 1771).

The interplay of mind and body is emphasized especially when Werther and Albert debate the morality of suicide: the conventional Albert condemns it as moral cowardice, the empathetic Werther imagines a suicidal disposition as a kind of illness, so that the suicide no more deserves blame than does an invalid who dies of fever. Such passages led the novel to be condemned as justifying or even glorifying suicide. It was claimed that the novel prompted a wave of copycat suicides, and the claim cannot be completely dismissed, for one young woman drowned herself in 1778 with a copy of *Werther* in her pocket. However, Goethe placed in the second edition of the novel (1775) some verses explicitly warning readers *not* to follow Werther's example. Even without them, it should have been clear that Werther's suicide results from his pathology, and also that, being accompanied by a long letter addressed to Lotte, it is an act both of violence towards himself and extreme emotional cruelty towards others. The novel as a whole is a balanced contribution to the late 18th-century debate on how suicide should be understood and judged now that many people no longer accepted the religious sanctions against it.

Werther as confession?

To place *Werther* in the history of 18th-century psychology is a salutary alternative to focusing on its biographical origins. However, Goethe's biography and personality are important. In the autobiography, *Aus meinem Leben: Dichtung und Wahrheit* (*From my Life: Poetry and Truth*), which he wrote largely between 1811 and 1814, he famously describes his works as 'fragments of a great confession'. We must treat this description with all due caution. He also tells us that throughout his life he would cope with his powerful feelings by transmuting them into an image. And it is clear both from his later autobiography and from contemporary testimony that the young Goethe felt disturbingly intense, barely controllable emotions which alternated between boisterous enthusiasm and restless melancholy. A poem written in uncertain English admits the 16-year-old's volatility: 'In Moments of Melancholy | Flies all my Happiness'. In the first emotional relationship that we know anything about for certain, with Käthchen Schönkopf, he tormented her with fantasies of jealousy, which she bore submissively till she finally rebelled and left him; he ruefully portrayed his own insufferable behaviour in the early play *Die Laune des Verliebten* (*The Lover's Moods*, 1767). He tells us in *Poetry and Truth* that he often thought about suicide.

So perhaps it is not surprising that *Werther* should be partly inspired by an actual suicide. On 29 October 1772 a young man called Karl Wilhelm Jerusalem, whom Goethe knew slightly, shot himself. The case attracted wide attention because Jerusalem's father was an eminent theologian and churchman. Goethe's friend Johann Christian Kestner sent him a detailed account of Jerusalem's unhappiness and death on 2 November 1772. Like Werther at court, Jerusalem had been unhappy in his work, and had suffered a social humiliation; he had an unrequited attachment to a married woman, whose husband forbade him to visit their house; he took long solitary walks through the woods at night; he borrowed pistols from Kestner and committed suicide in exactly the same way as Werther does in the novel, dressed in the blue coat and yellow waistcoat that Goethe would make into Werther's trademark costume. Even the last sentence of the novel, 'No priest attended', is taken from Kestner's letter.

Goethe's unabashed use of the Jerusalem material (what must the young man's bereaved parents have felt?) may be said to illustrate the egotism of genius. So does his treatment of the Kestners. Before her marriage to Kestner, Goethe had been warmly attached to Charlotte Buff, who has always been assumed to be the original of Werther's Lotte. The parallels are close, and Goethe even wrote an apologetic letter to the Kestners, forewarning them of their appearance in the novel. However, *Werther* is not a *roman à clef*, nor a disguised autobiography, and to identify fictional characters with real people is at best simplistic—though it provided an adequate pretext for Thomas Mann's fascinating novel, *Lotte in Weimar* (1939; known in English as *The Beloved Returns*), in which the widowed Lotte visits Goethe, now an elderly dignitary, in Weimar in 1816. What matters is the situation that Goethe's novel depicts: intense, unconsummated attraction to an unattainable woman.

This situation would recur several times in Goethe's life, the most famous example being the intimate friendship he enjoyed with the married Charlotte von Stein in Weimar from 1775 till his sudden departure for Italy in 1786. Even while writing *Werther* he was spending so much time with the newly married Maximiliane La Roche (daughter of the novelist Sophie La Roche) that her husband, a businessman twenty years her senior, became annoyed and may well have banned Goethe from the house. In 1775, for a change, Goethe fell in love with an accessible woman, Elisabeth ('Lili') Schönemann, daughter of a rich Frankfurt banker, but he felt that her smart social circle regarded him as an unconventional eccentric, an uncouth bear in Lili's menagerie (the image used in the poem 'Lilis Park'), and his unannounced departure on a trip to Switzerland in May 1775 may be seen as an escape from her.

Behind the women to whom Goethe was attracted although or because they were inaccessible, we can discern his sister Cornelia (1750–77). The siblings were deeply attached. Goethe describes Cornelia as unhappy, worried about her plainness, denied any education beyond the usual middle-class female accomplishments, and kept under surveillance by their well-meaning but strict and often authoritarian father. In 1773, much against her brother's will, she married the magistrate Johann Georg Schlosser (1739–99), but led a lonely and unhappy life with him. The constellation Goethe—Cornelia—Schlosser resembles the triangle Werther—Lotte—Albert. When Cornelia died in childbed in June 1777, Goethe was devastated. He wrote to his mother five months later: 'With my sister, such a strong root holding me to the earth has been chopped off, that the branches above, which should also have been nourished by it, must wither away.'

'This heart on fire'

Against this background, the early love poetry is rich in emotional complexity. A recurrent theme is the poet's need for someone to calm his turbulent emotions. It seems as if Goethe needed love, not to stimulate his passions, but to allay them. This is clear from a famous poem associated with Friederike Brion, a clergyman's daughter in the Alsatian village of Sesenheim, with whom Goethe had a relationship while studying in Strasbourg in 1770–1. Beyond the highly fictionalized account Goethe gave fifty years later in *Dichtung und Wahrheit*, we know little about Friederike; it is hard to guess how deep the relationship went, or why Goethe suddenly broke it off in August 1771. But we do not need such knowledge to appreciate the combination of energy and neediness in the poem beginning 'Mir schlug das Herz' (My heart beat), which Goethe wrote probably in 1771 and published first in 1775 and later, in a revised and (by common consent) enfeebled form, as 'Willkommen und Abschied' (Welcome and Departure). One evening the speaker suddenly resolves to ride off to visit his girl-friend: 'My heart beat: quick, to horse, | And away, wildly, like a hero to battle!' This feels excessively, disturbingly impetuous. On the nocturnal ride, the ghostly, sinister landscape seems to externalize the speaker's suppressed anxiety. His passion feels self-destructive: 'My spirit was a devouring fire, | My whole heart was melting in its glow.' When he meets his beloved, her 'gentle joy' calms him down. At their parting, she evidently walks back to her house, and he follows her with tearful looks: 'You went, I stood, and gazed at the ground, | And gazed after you with tears in my eyes'. The former hypermasculine hero is now a vulnerable and anxious person.

The need to be calmed persists after one of the great caesuras in Goethe's life, his move in November 1775 to the small court of Weimar, where, thanks to his celebrity, he was invited to be companion to the 18-year-old Duke Carl August. There he met, and rapidly fell in love with, Charlotte von Stein (1742–1827), wife of the Master of the Horse. A contemporary describes Charlotte as gentle, serious, with a refined sensibility and expressive dark eyes. Her marriage was probably unfulfilling; she and her husband often lived apart. At first she had to restrain Goethe's impetuosity, refusing for several years to let him address her by the intimate pronoun 'du', and exercising an authority enhanced by her noble status and her greater age. She thus ensured an attachment which lasted till Goethe's departure for Italy in 1786.

Early in their relationship, in April 1776, Goethe sent her the enigmatic, deeply personal poem 'Warum gabst du uns die tiefen Blicke' (Why did you give us deep insight), which he never published. If it portrays their relationship, it does so in fictionalized form, exploiting poetic licence to address her by the otherwise forbidden 'du'. She has calmed him: her intimate understanding of his character, conveyed in the psycho-physical terms we have come to expect, has quietened his impulsive blood and given direction to his aimless activity. But, and here the poem becomes deeply strange, this calming effect is said, employing the fiction of reincarnation, to have taken place during an earlier existence, when 'you were my sister or my wife'. In the present, the two live in a ghostly, twilit condition, with a self-knowledge denied to ordinary passionate lovers, enjoying a secure relationship whose centre is in the remote past.

Similarly subdued emotions are expressed in 'An den Mond' (To the Moon), a haunting poem which exists in three versions. The first, written perhaps in 1778, was not published in Goethe's lifetime. The second, published in 1789, is famous thanks to its settings by Schubert and numerous other composers. And the third was written by Charlotte von Stein, entitled 'To the Moon after my fashion', and possibly sent to Goethe to reproach him for his unannounced disappearance to Italy. A stanza from the first version is revealing:

> Das du so beweglich kennst,
> Dieses Herz in Brand,
> Haltet ihr wie ein Gespenst
> An den Fluß gebannt

> This heart on fire, which you know to be so volatile—the two of you hold it, like a ghost, bound to the river as by a spell.

The moon of the poem not only calms the speaker's fiery heart, but reduces him to a ghost-like state. It hints that Goethe found his relationship with Charlotte von Stein therapeutic, rewarding, but ultimately life-denying. Other evidence from his first decade in Weimar (1775–86) suggests that his many administrative burdens and his frustratingly platonic relationship with Charlotte hampered his creativity and made him ultimately desperate to escape. Having obtained permission from his employer, but without telling Charlotte, he slipped out of Carlsbad (the holiday resort in Bohemia to which some court members had migrated) at 3 a.m. on 3 September 1786. On 8 September he crossed the Brenner Pass into Italy, where he would spend the next two years.

Rome, Christiane Vulpius, and the creaking bed

Immediately after returning from Italy, Goethe set to work on what would prove one of his poetic masterpieces, the poetic cycle which he originally intended to call *Erotica Romana* but which eventually received the title *Römische Elegien* (*Roman Elegies*). Some of his friends in Weimar, alarmed by their sexual explicitness, dissuaded him from publishing them. It took his collaborator Friedrich Schiller (1759–1805), the great dramatist and philosopher, to see that their 'lofty poetic beauty' might offend against conventional prejudices, but not against 'that decency which is true and natural'. Twenty of the original twenty-four poems appeared in Schiller's periodical, *Die Horen* (*The Hours*, referring to the Greek goddesses of the seasons and hence of natural order), in June 1795 (the rest of the issue was taken up, not inappropriately, by Schiller's essay on the aesthetics of 'melting' or relaxing beauty). Set in modern Rome, the poems pay tribute to the Latin love-poets, especially Propertius, by adapting the elegiac distich in which a hexameter alternates with a pentameter. This may sound forbidding, but part of Goethe's achievement lies in adapting classical metres not only to a modern language but to the rhythms of the speaking voice.

The achievement of the *Elegies* is also to write frankly and seriously about a love-relationship that centres on physical enjoyment.

While the speaker celebrates the pleasure of being in Rome, away from grey northern skies, political gossip, and tedious questions about the facts behind *Werther*, he makes clear that antiquarian tourism would be no fun without the added pleasure of love. 'Roma' needs its palindrome 'Amor'. The relationship is both amorous and commercial. The speaker pays a young widow, called 'Faustina', for her sexual services, enabling her and her compliant mother to enjoy better food, clothes, and trips to the opera, and allowing him to enjoy sex without the fear of picking up a venereal disease from a prostitute. Faustina's wider family do not know about the relationship; she visits him at night, and is once nearly betrayed by a barking dog; when they happen to see each other in a restaurant, they can communicate only by secret signs. The poems convey the clandestine thrill of sharing a love-nest which the busy and prurient world knows nothing about. What happens there is robustly physical and also affectionate. The famous Elegy V describes how, after love-making and pillow-talk, she falls asleep and he taps out the rhythm of the hexameter on her back while watching her tenderly: 'She sweetly breathes in her slumber, | Warmly the glow of her breath pierces the depths of my heart.' In one of the poems that Goethe withheld from publication, the sparsely furnished bedroom becomes the setting for enjoyment worthy of the Roman gods, enhanced by the details of undressing and going to bed:

> We make short work of all that!—In a trice I unfasten this simple
> Woollen dress, and it drops, slips in its folds to the floor.
> Quickly, cajolingly, like a good nurse, I carry my darling—
> Only a light linen shift covers her now—to the bed.
> Here are no curtains of silk, no embroidered mattresses; freely
> In the wide bedroom it stands, ample in width to take two.
> Now not Jupiter's pleasure in Juno's embraces is greater,
> And no mortal's content vies, I will wager, with mine!
> Ours is the true, the authentic, the naked Love; and beneath us,
> Rocking in rhythm, the bed creaks the dear song of our joy.

The English-speaking reader inevitably recalls John Donne's elegy 'To his Mistress going to Bed':

> License my roving hands, and let them go
> Before, behind, between, above, below.

But, alongside the shared frankness, there are important differences between Donne and Goethe. The feverish intensity of Donne's poem differs from the happy fulfilment in Goethe's. Goethe evokes a mutual relationship, in which versions of 'we' occur three times, whereas Donne's poem throughout confronts an 'I' with a 'you' and uses the pronoun 'we' only as shorthand for 'we men'. Once again, in a more liberating way than in *Werther*, Goethe has extended the frontiers of what literature can express and, therefore, what its readers can experience.

What made this possible? The account of his stay in Italy, *Italienische Reise* (*Italian Journey*), which the elderly Goethe published in 1816–17, gives nothing away. Some think 'Faustina' never existed: after all, her name sounds like a playful invention by the author of *Faust*. However, archival evidence suggests that Goethe did have a clandestine love-relationship at least from January 1788, though his lover's real name cannot be established. Far from his accustomed surroundings and surveillance, Goethe may well have felt encouraged to kick over the traces.

If so, the effect was lasting. On 18 June Goethe was back in Weimar. On 12 July a 23-year-old woman named Christiane Vulpius, from an impoverished middle-class family, approached him in the Weimar park with a letter from her brother, a struggling writer. Goethe and Christiane became lovers, probably the same day. Their relationship, at first secret, soon became public knowledge, especially after the birth of their son August on 25 December 1789. For many years Goethe and Vulpius lived together as an unmarried couple—a scandal for the stuffy, hypocritical society of Weimar—marrying only in 1806 (see

Figure 4). The cheerful, warm-hearted, practical, domestic, devoted Christiane had much in common with Goethe's mother, who liked her and told Goethe: 'Such a dear, splendid, unspoiled creature of God is very hard to find.' There is no doubt that they were deeply happy together, that they had a fulfilling sexual relationship, and that Goethe felt grief amounting to despair after her death in 1816.

4. Christiane Vulpius, drawing by Goethe.

Goethe's sexual happiness with Christiane underlies not only the *Elegies* but also a later erotic poem, 'Das Tagebuch' (The Diary, 1810). This poem's sexual frankness caused consternation among Goethe's early editors: a toned-down version appeared only in 1861, the full text in 1914; the first English translation appeared in *Playboy* magazine in 1968. It is a narrative poem in Italian-style *ottava rima*. There are three characters: the narrator, a maidservant, and 'the Master'. The narrator is on a business trip when his carriage breaks down and he has to stay overnight in an inn. Distracted from writing to his wife by the beauty of the maidservant, he makes an assignation with her. But when she comes to his bedroom at midnight, the Master, also called 'Iste' (Latin, 'that one'), proves recalcitrant. This is the narrator's penis, which refuses an erection. Frustrated, the narrator recalls his joyful wedding night, and the many occasions when he and his wife have naughtily made love in the open air, and realizes that it is his intense emotional and physical attachment to his wife that causes erectile failure when he attempts adultery. The poem draws the moral conclusion that while duty can accomplish much, love can achieve infinitely more. It affirms a fidelity based on physical love, and implies, once again, that the human being is a psycho-physical unit, in which body, mind, and emotions all interact.

Marriage: *Elective Affinities*

Love, marriage and divorce are the subject of Goethe's novel *Die Wahlverwandtschaften* (*Elective Affinities*, 1809). They are treated with a frankness that shocked Goethe's readers in Victorian England: Thackeray in *Vanity Fair* deplores how in German society 'the *Wahlverwandtschaften* of Goethe is considered an edifying moral book'. The novel focuses on four characters: the aristocratic couple Eduard and Charlotte, their friend the Captain (later promoted to Major), and Charlotte's orphaned niece Ottilie. Its small cast, its setting on a country estate, its examination of relationships, the many discussions of moral, social, and emotional themes, and its frequent sly humour, recall Jane Austen. But, as a minor figure remarks, comedy treats marriage as the final goal, whereas in real life the action continues. Goethe's novel is about difficulties *after* marriage.

The novel treats marriage, not as a sacrament or a lifelong bond, but as a pragmatic social arrangement. In much of Germany, marriage was regulated by the Prussian legal code of 1794, which allowed divorce for many reasons, including no-fault divorce by mutual consent when a marriage was childless. Divorce carried no social stigma or legal disadvantages. Within the novel, a conservative attitude to marriage is voiced by the eccentric (and unmarried) Mittler, an amateur marriage counsellor, who maintains that marriage is the basis of civilization and that the unhappiness of individuals must not be allowed to weaken marriage as an institution. His opposite is another family friend, the Count, who proposes that marriage should be based on rolling five-year contracts.

Between these theories, the actual marriage of Eduard and Charlotte unfolds and unravels. Each is married for the second time. They were attracted to each other in their youth, but married other partners, who have since died. The impulsive, boyish Eduard and the sensible, self-controlled Charlotte seem to complement each other, but the fault-lines in their marriage are widened once the Captain and Ottilie join them. With many subtle and amusing psychological touches, Goethe charts the growth of love between Eduard and Ottilie, and between Charlotte and the Captain. It culminates in the episode that is later described as 'double adultery': Eduard and Charlotte make love, but he imagines embracing Ottilie, while she thinks about the Captain. (Had any previous novelist recorded the familiar but inadmissible fact that people have inappropriate thoughts while supposedly absorbed in love-making?) The next morning, Eduard and Charlotte feel guilty, while their house guests, the Count and his lover the Baroness, who are both married to other people, are relaxed after a night of joyful fornication. That evening, Eduard and Ottilie embrace—'It would not have been possible to say who first seized hold of the other' (I, xii)—and the Captain, helping Charlotte out of a boat, passionately kisses her.

How are we to explain the mystery of mutual attraction? The novel offers several explanatory models without definitely affirming any. Early on, in a famous conversation, the Captain explains to Eduard and Charlotte the nature of relationships among chemical elements: some are drawn to others by an innate similarity for which the technical term is 'elective affinity'; the addition of further elements can produce different combinations, making it seem as if the building-blocks of nature are driven either by a kind of agency, or by a higher necessity. Throughout the conversation, analogies are drawn with human relationships, implying that people, as part of the natural world, operate by a mixture of agency and necessity that defies analysis. Within the novel as a whole, Eduard's estate could be seen as a kind of human laboratory, where four people form different relationships under conditions of experimental purity. Moreover, all four have versions of the same name: the Captain is called Otto, Eduard was christened Otto but changed his name, and Charlotte and Ottilie share the syllable 'ott-'; and the name OTTO, composed of only two different letters, suggests a formula for the deep structure of human relationships.

Chemistry provides an analogy to human behaviour, but not an explanation. Eduard especially looks for other, providential signs that he and Ottilie are destined for each other. For example, a glass thrown into the air after a party is caught on the branch of a tree, and as it has the letters E and O on it, Eduard takes this to signify their eventual union. Again, some readers have detected sinister natural forces at work. The recurrent imagery of water, suggesting the fluidity and impermanence of social arrangements, appears especially with the lake on the estate, where several narrative turning-points (besides the Captain's kissing Charlotte) take place. However, nothing in the text actually requires a supernatural explanation. Such interpretations should be considered in the light of Eduard's statement: 'human beings are very narcissistic, they like to see themselves everywhere and be the foil for the rest of creation' (I, iv).

Although the chemical analogy may lead us to expect a smooth rearrangement of couples, that does not happen. Charlotte wants to save her marriage. Much as their parting pains her, she encourages the Captain to leave the estate for a job elsewhere. Eduard hopes that Charlotte will agree to a divorce, but that is ruled out when she reveals that she is pregnant. He leaves her, rejoins the army, and eventually returns with military decorations. By that time, their son has been born, and is christened Otto (what else?); and as the product of double adultery, the baby has the Captain's face and Ottilie's eyes. On his return, Eduard interprets this resemblance as yet further evidence that he and Ottilie were meant for each other. Ottilie agrees to marry him if a divorce makes it possible. With her emotions in turmoil after this encounter, she prepares to take the baby home by crossing the lake in a rowing-boat, but she loses control of the oars and drops the baby in the water. When she pulls him out, the baby is dead.

Long before this climactic scene, the novel has transferred its focus to Ottilie and begun building her up as a deeply sensitive and affectionate, even saintly figure. In a *tableau vivant* performed at Christmas, Ottilie represents the Virgin Mary, displaying not only her beauty but 'purest humility, the sweetest modesty in the receipt of a great and undeserved honour and of an inconceivably immeasurable happiness' (II, vi). This role contrasts tragically with her later attempt to revive the drowned baby by holding it to her breast. The catastrophe of the baby's death convinces Ottilie that in her attachment to Eduard she has strayed from her destined path, that God has opened her eyes to her wrong-doing, and that she must renounce Eduard and preserve his and Charlotte's marriage. The narrator supports Ottilie's mission by calling her 'the extraordinary child' and 'the heavenly child'. It is as though Ottilie, in a secular age when everyone else regards marriage as a merely social institution, has started a one-woman crusade to restore its religious meaning. To enforce its sanctity, Ottilie tells Charlotte that the moment she hears Charlotte has consented to a divorce, she, Ottilie, will drown herself. In her saintly conviction that she is doing God's will, Ottilie thus imposes her values on others by a monstrous piece of emotional blackmail.

Penitent martyr or moral tyrant? The enigma of Ottilie is deepened by the novel's end. She lives with Eduard and Charlotte, without speaking, and quietly starves herself to death. Her funeral is accompanied by an apparent miracle which is recounted with artful ambiguity. Eduard soon follows her into death, worn out by turbulent emotions. The two are buried in the same vault, united in death though not in life, and the last paragraph runs: 'So the lovers are side by side, at rest. Peace hovers over their dwelling-place, cheerful images of angels, their kith and kin, look down at them from the vaulted ceiling, and what a sweet moment it will be for their eyes when on some future day they awake together' (II, xviii). It was common in the 18th century to imagine loving couples as united in the next world, but Goethe (who had previously let Werther express an extravagant confidence in post-mortem union with Lotte) subtly varies the motif by making us wonder whether it is their love, or its renunciation, that wins the angels' goodwill, and whether their union, frustrated in this world, may be consummated in the hereafter.

Sublimation

Eduard's feelings for Ottilie acquire a religious tone. We are told that he dies thinking of 'the holy one' and may therefore be called 'blessed'. The elderly Goethe still writes love poetry, but love is increasingly sublimated into the contemplative, even devotional adoration of the beloved. In 1814 he formed an intense romantic friendship with the 30-year-old Marianne von Willemer, who had just become the third wife of a long-standing Frankfurt acquaintance of Goethe's, twenty years her senior. This was yet another attachment to an inaccessible woman. Goethe visited the couple in October 1814, and spent much of August and September 1815 with them, first in Frankfurt and then in Heidelberg. Marianne was a small, dark, vivacious, multi-talented woman, formerly a much-praised dancer; she sang her own poems and accompanied herself on the guitar. She and Goethe exchanged poems, assuming the Oriental identities of 'Zuleika' and 'Hatem'; Goethe later incorporated these poems into the *West-östlicher Divan* (*West-Eastern Divan*, 1819—to be discussed in Chapter 3), of which Marianne thus became co-author. A contemporary records a social evening where Goethe read poems aloud to the company while Marianne's husband fell asleep. In one of the most charmingly affectionate of the poems, Hatem contrasts Zuleika's brown curls with his own white hair, comparing himself to a snow-covered mountain illuminated by dawn:

> Du beschämst wie Morgenröte
> Jener Gipfel ernste Wand,
> Und noch einmal fühlet Hatem
> Frühlingshauch und Sommerbrand.
>
> You, like dawn, put to shame the grave cliff-face of those peaks, and once again Hatem feels the breath of spring and the burning heat of summer.

'Hatem' does not rhyme with 'Morgenröte' (dawn), but 'Goethe' does. By this little joke, Goethe hints at the emotions behind the poetic fiction, and, as elsewhere, uses rhyme to express the harmony between two lovers—for the dawn represents Marianne herself and the new life she has brought to a man in his mid-sixties. This new life, however, is imaginative rather than physical, and one poem spoken by Zuleika acknowledges that love must be sublimated into spiritual experience: 'For life is love, and the life of life is spirit.'

A stranger sublimation takes place in the 'Marienbader Elegie' (Marienbad Elegy), written in 1823 and published in 1827 as the centrepiece of 'Trilogie der Leidenschaft' (Trilogy of Passion). Over several successive summer holidays in the Bohemian resort of Marienbad, Goethe had got to know a young woman named Ulrike von Levetzow. In 1823 he proposed marriage to her. The 19-year-old Ulrike, encouraged by her mother to make her own decision, refused Goethe, less because of the 55-year age gap than because she felt unprepared for marriage (and, in her own retrospective account, feared the irritation of Goethe's son and daughter-in-law). On his journey home, Goethe worked through his emotions by composing a long farewell poem, in which the strict stanzaic form barely controls the powerful, often searingly painful feelings. At its climax, the poem dwells on the contemplation of the beloved:

> Dem Frieden Gottes, welcher euch hienieden
> Mehr als Vernunft beseliget—wir lesen's—,
> Vergleich' ich wohl der Liebe heitern Frieden
> In Gegenwart des allgeliebten Wesens;
> Da ruht das Herz, und nichts vermag zu stören
> Den tiefsten Sinn, den Sinn, ihr zu gehören.
>
> The peace of God, which for you on earth passes all understanding—so we read—, I can compare to the serene peace of love in the presence of the wholly beloved being; there the heart rests, and nothing can disturb the deepest sense, the sense of belonging to her.

The passage recalls the 'peace' which in much earlier poems Goethe attributes to the calming influence of a beloved woman.

If Goethe is supreme among love poets, it is because he explores so many aspects of an experience which in recent centuries has been considered central to human life. Other great love poets—Donne or Burns, or in German, Else Lasker-Schüler or Ingeborg Bachmann—render, however intensely, only a few notes in the scale; Goethe gives us the whole gamut, from youthful yearning via erotic fulfilment to late sublimation.

Chapter 2
Nature

Goethe, as we have seen, loved the idea of unity. For him there was no mind–body problem: the mind and the body were interlinked in innumerable ways, and the human being was a single whole combining both. Humanity, at the same time, formed part of a greater unity, that of nature.

Goethe's conviction that nature was unified and continuous can be traced back to the philosophy of Gottfried Wilhelm von Leibniz (1646–1716) in which nature is a single 'great chain of being', and to the principle 'nature makes no leaps', formulated by the pioneer of biological classification, Carl Linnaeus (1707–78), and reiterated by Goethe. However, this great unified nature was not only an object for philosophical reflection or scientific study. For Goethe, nature was also something to be experienced in the most direct, immediate way. And to grasp this experience, we need to look closely at a poem and appreciate, even with the help of translation, how Goethe's language expresses his sensuous apprehension of nature.

Auf dem See

Und frische Nahrung, neues Blut
Saug' ich aus freier Welt;
Wie ist Natur so hold und gut,
Die mich am Busen hält!

Die Welle wieget unsern Kahn
Im Rudertakt hinauf,
Und Berge, wolkig himmelan,
Begegnen unserm Lauf.

Aug', mein Aug', was sinkst du nieder?
Goldne Träume kommt ihr wieder?
Weg, du Traum! so Gold du bist;
Hier auch Lieb' und Leben ist.

Auf der Welle blinken
Tausend schwebende Sterne,
Weiche Nebel trinken
Rings die türmende Ferne;
Morgenwind umflügelt
Die beschattete Bucht,
Und im See bespiegelt
Sich die reifende Frucht.

On the Lake

And from this free world I suck fresh nourishment and new blood; how gracious and kindly is nature who holds me to her breast! The wave rocks our boat up and down in time with the oars, and mountains, cloudy skywards, meet our course. || Oh, my eyes, why are you drooping? Golden dreams, are you returning? Begone, you dream, golden as you are! There is love and life here too. || On the wave a thousand stars are glittering; soft clouds drink up the towering skyline; a breeze of morning flies round the shadowy bay, and in the lake is mirrored the ripening fruit.

Beginning abruptly with 'and', the poem plunges us into a particular experience. Goethe and his companions are being rowed across Lake Zurich early on the morning of 15 June 1775; he wrote the first version of the poem actually in the boat. Strong stresses and alliteration ('*W*elle *w*ieget') convey the regular, forceful motion of the boat. But the poem stresses the activity of their natural environment. The wave rocks the boat, and as the travellers approach the distant mountains, we are told that the mountains come to meet them. Most strikingly, the speaker is enfolded in maternal nature, like a child at the breast. The first version had him sucking nourishment through his umbilical cord, a process still hinted at in the first two lines of this version. The second section moves to slower, reflective trochees, recalling past dreams (of Goethe's ill-starred attachment to Lili Schönemann), only to dismiss them with renewed vigour. Now comes another change, to a delicate, semi-dactylic metre, as the boat nears the harbour and the morning advances. Natural phenomena are closely observed (as always in Goethe's engagement with nature): though the stars have vanished from the sky, their reflection is still visible in the lake; morning mists are rising, a breeze is getting up; the closeness of the bank is indicated indirectly by the fruit being reflected in the water. The language is not only intensely visual, but also tactile. The mists are soft, and the coinage 'umflügelt' (from *Flügel*, wing) conveys how the wind both seems to envelop the speaker and to touch his cheeks with feathery softness. These sensuous phenomena support a further, symbolic layer of meaning. The journey is not only from lake to land, from night to morning, but from birth and babyhood to maturity, signalled by the penultimate word 'ripening'.

Nature for Goethe is not only a sensuous maternal presence. In 1772, reviewing a treatise on aesthetics which called nature a 'tender mother', Goethe pointed to storms, floods, and volcanic eruptions, and asked what the author would say if Mother Nature were to swallow up a metropolis. Exactly that had happened in 1755, when an earthquake combined with a tsunami destroyed the city of Lisbon, killing, according to Goethe's estimate, some 60,000 people. Werther, in gloomy moods, sees nature as a destructive monster. In the poem 'Das Göttliche' (The Divine), Goethe rejects the pathetic fallacy which attributes our emotions to nature: 'For nature is unfeeling.' Most often, Goethe imagines nature as above all dynamic—constantly in motion, both creative and destructive. When Faust summons up the Earth Spirit, the embodiment of nature, the spirit is too powerful for the would-be magician to handle: 'In life like a flood, in deeds like a storm | I surge to and fro, | Up and down I flow! | Birth and the grave | An eternal wave, | Turning, returning, | A life ever burning' (lines 504–7) (see Figure 5). As a living, dynamic, ever-changing force, nature can never be adequately described, so the language used for it must always be provisional and, even at its most sober, have something of the metaphorical quality of poetry.

Goethe repeatedly asserted that he owed his understanding of nature especially to the Dutch–Jewish philosopher Baruch Spinoza (1632–77). He read Spinoza's *Ethics* mainly in 1773–4 and 1784–5, though in 1815 he claimed that he always carried the book around with him. This taste showed Goethe's independence of mind, for Spinoza, who in 1656 had been formally expelled from his own community for supposed atheism, had an equally bad reputation among orthodox Christians. Spinoza's God is not a person with feelings, but an infinite and necessary being. As God is infinite, everything that exists is within God: hence Spinoza speaks of 'that eternal and infinite being we call God, or nature'. God is equally within nature. Hence Goethe, in a late poem, could ask: 'What sort of God would it be who pushed the universe from outside and rotated it with his finger? It befits Him to move the world from within, to cherish nature in Himself and Himself in nature.' Believing that all things are necessary, Spinoza denies that anything is bad in itself, though it may appear so in our imaginations. 'Nature is always right,' Goethe told his secretary Eckermann on 13 February 1829, 'and the mistakes and errors are always made by humans.' This confirmed the view of nature that Goethe had already expressed in 1772: 'What we see of nature is energy that consumes energy, nothing static, everything transient, a thousand seeds crushed every minute and a thousand born, great and momentous, infinitely various; beautiful and ugly, good and evil, everything existing with an equal right alongside everything else.'

5. The Earth Spirit appearing to Faust, drawing by Goethe.

Finally, Goethe quotes from Spinoza the claim that the highest form of knowledge is intuitive (*scientia intuitiva*), and adds: 'these few words give me courage to devote my life to the contemplation of things that are within my reach'. Goethe here slips between intellectual apprehension and visual sight, telling his pious correspondent: 'When you say one can only *believe* in God, I set great store by *seeing*.' Hence, as we shall soon see, the highest aim of Goethe's researches was not the abstract reflection on nature, but its intelligent contemplation, for which he favours the word *Anschauen*. And hence, too, Goethe seems to have recruited Spinoza to support his own, intensely visual experience of the world. 'The eye', he wrote in his autobiography, 'was above all others the organ by which I apprehended the world.'

Goethe's study of nature

The study of nature has to begin with the phenomena (a favourite word of Goethe's), the natural objects that are present to our senses. For Goethe, who had an acute and vivid sense of sight, this means above all the objects that we see. In the diary that he wrote for Charlotte von Stein during his first weeks in Italy, he recalls on 9 October 1786 how that afternoon he watched sea-snails and crabs in the Venetian lagoon: 'how delightful and magnificent a *living thing* is! How exactly matched to its condition, how true, how intensely *being*!' The investigator had to hold on to this intensely *being* quality of nature; otherwise he risked slipping from phenomena to mere words, and from words to abstractions.

Given his fear of abstraction, Goethe was inevitably hostile to the most successful model of scientific research in his time: the conception of the universe as a great machine, operating by regular laws, and capable of being described in quantitative and mathematical terms. Goethe knew little of mathematics: in 1786 he tried to learn algebra, with limited success. He says that mathematics is all very well in its place, dealing with those restricted areas where exactitude is possible, but should abandon its claim to 'universal monarchy'. The study of nature needs to emancipate itself from mathematics and 'seek with all loving, reverent, devout energies to penetrate nature and its holy life'. Although he occasionally used a microscope to examine micro-organisms, and enjoyed looking at the moon through a telescope, Goethe generally deplored the use of instruments such as microscopes and telescopes, on the grounds that they distorted the natural relation between the observer and the world.

Despite rejecting mathematical abstraction, Goethe did not confine himself to the empirical study of phenomena. He cogently criticized the experimental method advocated early in the 17th century by Francis Bacon and practised after 1660 by the Royal

Society in London. Empirical studies need to be guided by principles, otherwise they will just lead to millions of isolated and insignificant facts. The Royal Society, though claiming to study nature without preconceptions, in fact assumed that the universe was really a great machine. The investigator, in Goethe's view, needed to remember that there were no raw facts, independent of the viewer's preconceptions.

However, when Goethe writes: 'The supreme goal would be to grasp that everything factual is already theory', he does not mean 'theory' in any recognizable present-day sense. He rejects 'theory' in the sense of mathematical abstraction. Nor has he any interest in causal explanations for phenomena. After all, since everything in nature is interrelated, a causal account merely privileges *one* set of relationships, a historical one, at the expense of innumerable others. Often he uses the word 'theory' in the original sense of the Greek *theoria*, meaning 'looking'. This brings us back to the contemplation or *Anschauen* that Goethe learnt from Spinoza. Ultimately, all you can do with phenomena is to contemplate them. There is nothing behind them, nothing to be explained. The aphorism just quoted continues: 'The blue of the sky reveals to us the basic law of chromatics. Do not look for anything behind the phenomena: they themselves are the doctrine.' Even to express phenomena in words requires caution, since language is just another phenomenon; we must use language with self-awareness and irony if we are not to fall into mere abstraction.

Does this mean that all the scientist can do is to gaze raptly at nature? Hardly; there is plenty to be found out about the workings of natural phenomena: about the anatomy of living creatures, the growth of plants, the production of colours, and the formation of geological strata—all matters which Goethe investigated in great detail. Such studies, keeping close to the sensuous reality of phenomena, permit generalizations and ultimately lead one to a higher order of phenomena: what Goethe calls the 'primal phenomenon' (*Urphänomen*). Here is Goethe's account of scientific method:

> What we become aware of in experience is mostly just individual cases, which, with close attention, can be subsumed under general empirical categories. These in turn are subordinated to scientific categories, which point us further, making us acquainted with certain indispensable conditions of the phenomenon. Henceforth everything gradually arranges itself under higher rules and laws, which reveal themselves, not through words and hypotheses to the intellect, but through phenomena to contemplation (*Anschauen*). We call them *Urphänomene*, because in the phenomenal world there is nothing above them; but just as we have ascended to them step by step, so we can descend from them to the commonest case of everyday experience.

Thus the *Urphänomen* is a kind of limit case in nature. The magnet is an *Urphänomen*; light is another; so is granite, as the oldest and most basic kind of rock. The *Urphänomen* cannot be explained or analysed. It just is itself. But it does belong to a category, and is an exceptionally striking member of that category, revealing the quality common to all instances. By arranging other instances—rock types, for instance—in an orderly sequence related to the *Urphänomen*, the investigator can arrive at valid generalizations which are available to contemplation with the minimum of abstraction.

However sympathetically we try to reconstruct it, Goethe's scientific method remains at best problematic. The *Urphänomen* seems to be envisaged as a kind of Platonic form, or universal type, which however does not exist in another, ideal realm, but is available as part of experience. In a famous conversation with Schiller, Goethe described the *Urpflanze* or primal plant—another *Urphänomen*, which he had hoped to find in the gardens at Palermo. Schiller, who was an astute philosopher, replied: 'That isn't an experience;

it's an idea.' Schiller understood the distinction between regulative ideas, which help us make sense of experiences, and the experiences themselves. Goethe replied good-humouredly: 'Well, I'm glad I have ideas without knowing it, and can even see them.' But Schiller was right. The attractive but untenable concept of the *Urphänomen* cannot really provide an alternative to abstraction in the study of nature.

Goethe's understanding of nature does, all the same, rely on abstract concepts. He became increasingly convinced that nature consists of two opposing principles, reconciled within a greater unity. For this concept of 'polarity' he gave credit to Immanuel Kant, having read in the latter's *Metaphysical Bases of Natural Science* (1786) that all matter is moved by two contrary forces, attraction and repulsion. Goethe finds polarities everywhere: light and darkness, spirit and matter, imagination and reason, systole and diastole (the alternate contraction and dilation of the heart). Another concept Goethe favours is that of *Steigerung* or intensification: a struggle towards perfection which governs the development of each organism. Goethe uses *Steigerung* very broadly, applying it, for example, to personal development, to the upward growth of a plant, and to the transition from a republic to an aristocracy. In the last letter he ever wrote, the spirited 82-year-old declares: 'I have no more urgent task than to intensify [*steigern*] what remains to me, and to distil my individuality further.' Clearly 'intensify' is as much a metaphor as 'distil', illustrating Goethe's assumption that our language about nature is always ultimately metaphorical.

Goethe developed these notions partly through discussion with Romantic philosophers, particularly F. W. J. Schelling (1775–1854), who made a great impact while holding a professorship at the University of Jena, near Weimar, in 1798–1803. However, these ideas, despite their powerful appeal to the imagination, are not scientific concepts. They are rather a metaphysics of nature, which cannot be demonstrated and which is independent of scientific research. Accordingly, they find their most memorable expression in the poems which Goethe published under the heading 'God and World' in the edition of his works which he supervised before his death.

Goethe's study of nature follows philosophical conceptions, derived ultimately from Plato and Leibniz, which are remote from present-day science. His rejection of mathematics and his disapproval of scientific instruments leave little scope for scientific discovery. That would not have worried Goethe. He did not think there was a great deal to be discovered. 'Much more has already been discovered than people realize', he wrote. The history of science was for him not a linear development but a spiral movement in which similar ideas reappeared on different levels. Hence science needed to be aware of its own history. Scientific views often differed, not in substance, but in the outlooks of their proponents. Ultimately, they expressed their proponents' individuality: 'only the whole of humanity can understand nature' (letter to Schiller, 5 May 1798). Hence there should be toleration of different scientific views, just as in New York ninety different Christian denominations were tolerated.

Morphology

From the early 1780s Goethe gave much energy to what would later be called biology or the life sciences. For this pursuit he coined in 1796 the word 'morphology', meaning the study of living forms. He was guided by his conviction of the unity and continuity of nature. This conviction prompted what is widely regarded as his one actual scientific discovery, that of the intermaxillary bone in humans. Most mammals have an upper jaw consisting of two bones on either side, together forming the maxilla or jawbone, and separated by the frontal intermaxillary bone, in which the incisor teeth are set. The intermaxillary bone is marked by three sutures.

In adult humans, the intermaxillary bone is fused with the jaw, but in embryos and sometimes in children's skulls the two outer sutures can still be detected by a keen observer, and Goethe perceived them in 1784. This was for him an exciting discovery, because it confirmed that humanity had the same physical equipment (albeit here in extremely residual form) as the rest of the animal kingdom. Humanity was indeed part of nature, not (as the pious claimed) a distinct reality specially created by God. Unfortunately, Goethe's discovery (which anyway had already been made by the French physiologist Félix Vicq d'Azyr) was received sceptically by his fellow-scientists, and he did not publish it until 1820.

Undeterred, Goethe persisted with anatomy and botany, guided by the concepts of 'metamorphosis' and the 'type'. He set out his ideas not only in treatises such as *Versuch, die Metamorphose der Pflanzen zu erklären* (*An Attempt to Explain the Metamorphosis of Plants*, 1790) but also in two didactic poems, 'The Metamorphosis of Plants' (1798) and 'Metamorphosis of Animals' (published 1820 but written perhaps in 1806). In using poetry, he was following the example of the Roman poet Lucretius, who had described the physical universe and the natural world in his poem *De rerum natura* (*On the Nature of the Universe*, 1st century BCE). It was still common in the 18th century to write about scientific topics in verse, as in the poetic account of plant reproduction, *The Loves of the Plants* (1791), by Erasmus Darwin (grandfather of Charles).

The two poems, however, describe very different kinds of metamorphosis. The poem on plants recounts in loving detail the transformation undergone by a plant from the seed to the flower, from which, in a continual cycle, new seeds and hence new plants are generated. Goethe claims (more explicitly in the *Versuch*) that the seed first produces a leaf and that every organ the plant subsequently develops (petals, stamens, pistils) is a variation on the leaf. Thus the plant retains unity throughout its metamorphoses.

Goethe's understanding of animal development, however, stemmed from seeing a sheep's skull on the Venetian Lido in 1790, which brought him the sudden conviction that an animal's skeletal structure, including the bones of the skull or cranium, is a series of variations on the vertebra. Moreover, the development of an animal's body is subject to a law of compensation, whereby the growth of one organ means the disappearance of another: thus animals with massive teeth lack the material to develop horns—'And it would therefore be completely impossible for the eternal Mother to form a horned lion, however hard she tried.' Charles Darwin acknowledges Goethe's theory in *The Origin of Species* (1859), but explains the apparent law, insofar as it exists, from the economy of nature: when an animal's conditions of life change and an organ is no longer useful, natural selection gradually eliminates it.

More problematic is the concept of the underlying model or type. Goethe does not mean that animals' skeletons develop from the skull. He means that they are variations on a basic prototype. But in what sense does this prototype exist? Some 18th-century naturalists spoke of the 'type' as a kind of Platonic form, existing in an ideal realm, and Goethe follows this tradition when he suggests that the type is an idea existing in the mind of God/nature. These notions are very remote from Darwin. Neither of Goethe's conceptions of metamorphosis anticipates Darwinian evolution. Like other 18th-century thinkers, who had no idea of the innumerable extinct varieties that the fossil record would reveal, Goethe thought that species were fixed. He acknowledged some scope for mutability only when he accepted that the skeleton of a giant bull, dug up near Stuttgart, might represent an ancestor of the smaller modern oxen. Goethe's work on anatomy and botany included his main contributions to scientific knowledge; but some of it was based on assumptions which were soon to become obsolete and even unintelligible.

Geology

Goethe's interest in geology originated from practical requirements. Some fifteen months after his arrival in Weimar, the Duke gave him the task of overseeing the restoration of the silver mine at nearby Ilmenau, in the hope of saving the Duchy from the threat of bankruptcy. The project was ill-starred: it went over budget; a new shaft was sunk in 1784, but flooded in 1796; the mine was finally closed in 1812. However, Goethe became fascinated by mineralogy and geology. He made a large collection of mineral samples. And he took a keen interest in theories about the formation of the earth's surface.

The dominant theory in the late 18th century was Neptunism. It was upheld especially by Abraham Gottlob Werner (1750–1817), professor at the important mining academy at Freiberg in Saxony, whom Goethe knew personally. Werner was a major scientist; by studying successive rock formations, he worked out some of the geological periods that are still recognized today. His Neptunist theory, however, has not stood the test of time. It maintained that originally the whole earth was covered by water; that chemicals in the water crystallized to form the earth's crust, beginning with granite, which was therefore the most ancient rock; that as the ocean level sank, the rocks were exposed and eroded, and the products of erosion formed the more recent geological strata. This theory appealed to Goethe's conviction that nature worked in a slow, continuous manner. He disliked the violent upheavals proposed by the rival, Vulcanist theory, which argued that the earth's core contained intense heat which impelled volcanic activity by which the surface of the earth was heaved up to form mountains. Since even scientists in the 18th century thought the earth might at most be a hundred thousand years old, this implied sudden, horrific cataclysms, not the imperceptibly slow process by which we now know mountains were formed.

Vulcanism (supplemented by elements of Neptunism to account for sedimentary rocks) eventually carried the day, thanks in part to the truly pioneering scientist Alexander von Humboldt (1769–1859), who had observed the results of volcanic activity in South America, and who, despite his respect for Goethe, deplored the latter's 'geological fantasies'. Goethe, though unwilling to acknowledge volcanic activity except at a recent stage in the earth's formation, admitted late in life that Humboldt's case for Vulcanism was persuasive, but found it as unintelligible as a religious mystery: 'That the Himalayas were raised 25,000 feet from the ground, yet project skywards as solidly and proudly as though nothing had happened, is beyond the limits of my head, in the gloomy regions where transubstantiation and such things dwell, and my whole cerebral system would have to be restructured—which would be a shame—in order to find room for such miracles'.

Goethe's approach to geology finds expression in some literary works. In *Faust II*, he satirizes Vulcanism by making the Devil a Vulcanist. Much earlier, in 1784, he wrote a lyrical essay celebrating granite as the foundation of the earth; it may have been intended as part of the prose 'romance about the universe' that he conceived (but did not write) at this time (letter to Charlotte von Stein, 7 December 1781). Seated on a bare granite hilltop in the Harz Mountains, he imagines how it may have projected from the waters that originally covered the earth, how primitive life-forms, first mosses and then marine shellfish, appeared in succession, how the waters retreated and the newly exposed land became covered with vegetation. Raging volcanoes may have thrust themselves up, but they had no effect on the solid, immemorial granite. Whether such writing is scientifically accurate hardly matters: it enriches our awareness of the world around us.

The doctrine of colours

Goethe was led by his interest in painting to the study of colour and thus to the longest book he ever published, *Zur Farbenlehre*

(*On the Doctrine of Colours*, 1810; 'doctrine' conveys better than 'theory' the quasi-religious conviction that animates it). The standard account of the origin of colours had been provided by Isaac Newton on the basis of an experiment conducted in 1666 and described in Newton's *Opticks* (1704). Newton assumed that the white light from the sun was a mixture of rays, which were themselves made up of particles. When they pass through a prism, rays bend at different angles, depending on the weight of the particles composing them. These differences in refraction create the various colours that appear in the rainbow: red, at one end of the spectrum, bends least; violet, at the other extreme, bends most. In his crucial experiment, Newton set up a prism near his window and projected a spectrum onto the far wall.

Goethe could not accept that colours were produced by the varying refrangibility of rays. Such an explanation meant that colours were not a real part of experience, but merely a subjective by-product of a physical process which could best be described in quantitative terms. This was antithetical to Goethe's belief in the reality of phenomena. Moreover, when he tried to reproduce Newton's experiment, he found that no spectrum appeared on the wall; a colour was only visible when close to something dark. With the help of many further experiments, Goethe arrived at a theory in which colour was produced by the polarity of light and darkness and by an intermediate semi-translucent medium. Thus the light of the sun reaches us through the atmosphere, which, as a thin medium, shows the sun as yellow; a denser medium, such as various kinds of vapour or atmospheric pollution, shows it as red. Some colours, such as yellow, are modifications of light, others, such as its polar opposite blue, of darkness. Different shades of colour result from intensification (*Steigerung*) of these basic colours, or from their combination, as when yellow and blue together make green.

The eye does not merely register colours, but contributes actively to their production. Early in his treatise, Goethe adapts the saying of the Neoplatonic mystic Plotinus: 'If the eye were not sun-like, how could we perceive light?' Light has an internal, as well as an external source; otherwise, Goethe strangely argues, how could we see in our dreams? We virtually never experience white light. Light is always coloured, and colours are closely linked to our emotions. Yellow and its derivatives are stimulating; blue and its derivatives induce a restless, yearning mood; green is restful. Our innate need for a totality makes us seek harmonies among colours. But the totality of colours is never available in nature—even the rainbow does not include purple, which Goethe considers the chief among colours—so we need art to satisfy our colour sense fully.

In setting this account against Newton's, Goethe felt that he was attacking an orthodoxy which had become despotic. He compares Newton's colour theory to an old dilapidated fortress like the Bastille that needed to be razed to the ground. But his obsessive, sometimes scurrilous campaign against Newton was inevitably unsuccessful. Although Goethe made some valid methodological criticisms of Newton for confusing fact and theory, e.g. in talking of rays as real entities rather than theoretical constructs, these criticisms missed the main point. Newton's account of the spectrum remains substantially valid. Goethe's essay is a quixotic rearguard action against the mathematization of science.

Presenting the *Doctrine of Colours* to an English readership, his translator prudently suggested that, whatever its scientific flaws, its reflections on colour harmony would be valuable for painters. J. M. W. Turner read it, and though his annotations are sceptical, he paid it qualified homage by giving the title *Light and Colour (Goethe's Theory)—the Morning after the Deluge—Moses writing the Book of Genesis* (1843) to a painting dominated by a swirling yellow vortex. Later, in Switzerland, Wassily Kandinsky found Goethe's remarks on the psychological effects of colours suggestive for his own treatise *On the Spiritual in Art* (1911).

Was Goethe a scientist?

Goethe devoted as much or more time to studying the natural world as he did to literature. His study of nature is inspiring in its loving attention to detail and in its ambitious attempt to grasp nature as a whole through such concepts as 'polarity'. It can and should send us back to look at the natural world around us with fresh eyes and increased appreciation, wonder, even reverence.

But does that make it science? Science aims to give an accurate account of the physical world by framing hypotheses, testing them in experiments, and arriving at general laws which explain the workings of nature. Goethe aimed to move from particular phenomena to the contemplation of irreducible, inexplicable *Urphänomene*. He rejected abstraction, avoided mathematics, and even disapproved of using scientific instruments to see more than the unaided senses could perceive. He was a reliable observer, took a serious part in scientific discussions, and made a discovery in human anatomy; his work on plant metamorphosis, in particular, was found valuable by botanists down to the 20th century. But although he says that a scientist should be as neutral as a juryman, he tended in practice to adopt scientific theories, such as Neptunism, because they appealed to him, or to reject them, as with Newton's spectrum, because they were uncongenial. His principles set very narrow limits to what science can discover. For example, our unaided senses could not tell us that matter is composed of atoms; and here Goethe falls behind the ancient Greeks, who had an atomic theory, although they had no way of testing it.

On the other hand, it might be argued that Goethe was a scientist, but of a different kind. It is now widely held that science does not progress in a straight line, with one fact after another being added; rather, it undergoes periodical paradigm shifts, in which a new, epoch-making discovery, such as Newton's theory of gravity or Darwin's theory of evolution, forces scientists to rethink basic assumptions and to discard or reinterpret much that they thought they knew. So we might say that Goethe was a scientist working in an older, pre-Newtonian paradigm, whose goal was to find and contemplate real manifestations of Platonic forms. But, leaving aside the difficulties of this conception, such a paradigm would still allow very limited scope for new discoveries. Much of the work done under such a paradigm would look, from a present-day perspective, less like natural science than like natural history—a discipline that aims not to explain natural phenomena by general laws, but simply to describe them. Even so, Goethe's empirical studies of botany, colour perception, and other subjects provided much valuable material for later generations. And while his dislike of abstraction set limits to his science, it was the counterpart of one of his greatest gifts—his intense awareness of the physical presence of objects, whether natural or artistic. 'You know how the presence of things speaks to me,' he wrote to Charlotte von Stein from Italy in September 1786, 'and here I'm in conversation with things all day long.'

Since he thought nature was a perpetual flux which always eludes our grasp, Goethe rejected the functional precision of scientific language in favour of a suggestive, metaphorical style, which enormously benefits his literary work. Metaphor and analogy enable him to suggest innumerable relationships between human life and the natural world in which it is embedded. In the last chapter we saw how the novel *Elective Affinities* takes its title from a concept in chemistry. That does not mean that Goethe is using chemistry to explain human relations; rather, he is suggesting an analogy between chemical and human pairings, in order to convey freshly how much in human behaviour, including some life-changing decisions, comes from our physical being, below the level of consciousness. In literature he can practise irony and ambiguity, which correspond to his sense that human life and the natural world are ultimately mysterious and that the scientific desire to 'explain' is often over-hasty, leading us away from the manifold implications of experience.

Nature and literature: *Wilhelm Meister's Apprenticeship*

To see how this works in practice, let us look briefly at how the language of nature is used in the long novel, *Wilhelm Meisters Lehrjahre* (*Wilhelm Meister's Apprenticeship*), which Goethe published in 1795–6, at the period of his most intense studies of morphology. In the early 1780s Goethe had written an unfinished novel, *Wilhelm Meisters theatralische Sendung* (*Wilhelm Meister's Theatrical Mission*), in which a young middle-class German is so stage-struck that he leaves his dull business career, takes up with a troupe of travelling actors, and then joins a professional theatre company based in Hamburg. Returning to the novel ten years later, Goethe toned down its lively, sometimes knockabout realism and took the story in a different direction. Wilhelm now finds that his life is being supervised by a secret society, the Society of the Tower, which eventually draws him away from the theatre and gives him a place in a community of social reformers. To get there, however, Wilhelm not only makes a long detour via his unsuccessful theatrical career, but also goes through a series of unhappy love-affairs. The Society finally unites him with his destined partner, the good, intelligent, and beautiful Natalie, whom he has been semi-consciously seeking ever since an earlier chance encounter.

The novel's key words include *bilden* (to form) and *Bildung*, which can be translated as 'formation', 'cultivation', or 'education'. It therefore has a special status as the archetypal 'Bildungsroman' or 'novel of education', though Goethe did not use this term and it was applied to *Meister* and similar novels only retrospectively in the late 19th century. In his biological writings, Goethe speaks of a 'bildende Kraft' or shaping force that guides the development of an organism. So in some ways Wilhelm's development may be compared to the growth of a plant, unconsciously seeking to flower and reproduce.

This of course is an analogy, not an equivalence. Human beings can also undergo 'Bildung' in the sense of education, and the members of the Society have different views on how to educate Wilhelm. Jarno, a military officer, thinks that when people are going astray, you should bluntly set them right, and so he rebukes Wilhelm for wasting his time with the actors; whereas the Abbé, an enlightened priest much influenced by Rousseau's progressive ideas on education, thinks that you should let people make their own mistakes and trust to nature to teach them wisdom. This seems to work, for Wilhelm tires of the theatre on realizing that his acting talent is confined to representing characters who resemble himself. Wilhelm has yet another notion, for half-way through he writes to a friend that he seeks 'the harmonious development [*Ausbildung*] of my nature' (V, 3); but he imagines that he can best do this by becoming an actor, a plan he soon abandons. In the end, he is not a harmonious, rounded person, but a one-sided individual, just like the Society's other members: some are practical, one is religious, Natalie is committed to good works but indifferent to art. A spokesman concludes: 'All humans make up humanity and all forces together make up the world. These are often in conflict with each other, and while they are trying to destroy each other nature holds them together and creates them anew' (VIII, 5). Human society is shaped and guided by nature.

Wilhelm's development is tortuous and crisis-ridden. He continually misunderstands his situation, and often, accidentally and unwittingly, inflicts suffering on others. To the Society, with its upbeat view of life, these are 'errors' and 'follies' from which he should move on (VII, 9). He finds deep satisfaction in caring for the mysterious child Mignon, who treats him as a surrogate father; and later he finds that he is really a father, for his lover, Mariane, whom he abandoned (wrongly believing her to be unfaithful) and who died in poverty, bore him a child, whom after her death he has to care for. He takes delight in this task. Responsibility for his son makes him plan for the future. Thus, despite escaping from his middle-class background, he has acquired by a natural process all the middle-class virtues.

'How unnecessary is the strictness of morality,' he exclaimed, 'when nature, in her own pleasant way, makes us into everything that we should be. How strange are the demands of society that confuse and mislead us, finally demanding more from us than nature herself. I deplore all attempts at developing us which destroy the most effective means of education [*Bildung*] by forcing us towards the goal instead of giving us a sense of happiness along the way' (VIII, 1).

However inviting these views about nature and education may be, we have to remember that the novel does not present them as doctrine. They are uttered by fictional characters, whose beliefs qualify each other and may change at a later stage. Thus Goethe is an ironic novelist: not in undermining his own apparent assertions, but in composing his novel in such a way that no statement is the complete truth. On its central themes of nature and education, the novel offers a variety of perspectives which do not undercut but enrich one another, discouraging us from the hasty search for a final answer.

Chapter 3
Classical art and world literature

The visual arts were as important to Goethe as literature. As a young man he was unsure whether to become a poet or a painter. Until 1788 he probably spent more time sketching, and learning other artistic techniques, than he spent writing, and during his two-year stay in Italy he devoted himself whole-heartedly to the study and practice of the visual arts, though he found time also to complete the still unfinished literary works that he had brought with him.

Goethe's knowledge of art and literature was wide-ranging, but in both he came to believe that the works produced by the ancient Greeks formed a standard that could never be surpassed. In art he explored especially the classical tradition that descended via the Renaissance to the neoclassicism of the 18th century. In literature, though he read and studied Homer intensively, his taste was much wider. Not only did he read easily in French, Italian, and English as well as Latin and Greek, but as a young man we find him acquiring scraps of Gaelic in order to appreciate Ossian and exploring Serbian ballads, while in his later life he eagerly read translations of the Asian texts that scholars were making available to Europe—novels from China, epics and plays from India, and, above all, the Arabic and Persian poetry that would inspire his great lyrical collection, the *West-östlicher Divan* (*West-Eastern Divan*, a 'divan' being a collection of poetry).

Goethe and visual art

The German language distinguishes *Augenmenschen* (eye-people) and *Ohrenmenschen* (ear-people). Although Goethe appreciated music, and was a competent pianist, he was emphatically an *Augenmensch*. He was also from an early age familiar with painters. His father commissioned many paintings from local Frankfurt artists, whom the young Goethe saw at work and got to know. Goethe came to see the world with a painterly eye: he speaks of 'my tendency to look at the world through the eyes of the painter whose pictures I have seen last' (*Italian Journey*, 8 October 1786). Hence in Venice, crossing the lagoon in brilliant sunshine, he felt as though he were looking at a bright and colourful Venetian painting.

Might Goethe himself have become a major artist? It is unlikely. His sketches, of which some 3,000 survive, are talented and sensitive, but he himself admitted their lack of 'creative power', and late in life he described them as insubstantial: 'I had a certain fear of letting the objects make their full impact on me', he told Eckermann (10 April 1829). In his fictional conversation about art, 'The Collector and his Circle' (1799), he characterized a type of artist, the 'sketcher', who addresses the spirit rather than the senses: Art should not speak only through the external senses to the mind, it should also satisfy the senses. Then the mind may participate and grant its approval. But the Sketcher addresses the mind directly, thereby seducing and delighting inexperienced people.

It was essential for Goethe that art should be solid, substantial, and satisfying to the eye. In his youth, encouraged by the Frankfurt artists, he preferred the realism of Dutch painting, as opposed to the often playful, extravagant, other-worldly style of the many Baroque churches and palaces throughout southern Germany. The quality he admired was truth to nature, as when Rembrandt, in *The Adoration of the Shepherds*, shows the Holy

Family in a convincingly humble stable, which the shepherds are entering with the help of a lantern.

Of Goethe's early writings on art, however, the most original and the most untypical is his lyrical essay on Strasbourg Cathedral, published in 1772 as 'On German Architecture', and dedicated to the memory of the medieval architect Erwin von Steinbach. At a time when Gothic architecture was still generally thought to be barbarous, Goethe perceived the harmony and proportion underlying the cathedral's apparent disorder. It had the same kind of unity as a natural organism: 'As in the works of eternal nature, everything is formed, down to the merest thread, and everything serves a purpose in relation to the whole.' In seeing great art as shaped by natural laws, Goethe was here anticipating a major theme of his later aesthetic writings. But in celebrating the cathedral as proceeding from 'a strong, rugged German soul', and mistakenly assuming that Gothic art originated in Germany, Goethe was voicing a nationalism that flourished in 1770s Germany, in reaction against the excessive prestige of French culture, but that he would ever afterwards oppose. 'Of German Architecture' is a dead end in his works, for he never again wrote about medieval architecture, but it was a path-breaking and influential text in the revival of interest in Gothic architecture pioneered by the Romantics and put into practice by such Victorian architects as Augustus Pugin (1812–52).

Classicism

Goethe's visit to Italy in 1786–8 marked a turning-point in his life in many ways—not least in his appreciation of art. Living amid Roman remains and Renaissance masterpieces, Goethe was converted to classicism: all artistic greatness came ultimately from ancient Greece.

The enthusiasm for the Greeks that seized late 18th-century Germany has been called 'the tyranny of Greece over Germany', but might rather be described as the liberating influence of a foreign culture. It goes back to the art historian Johann Joachim Winckelmann (1717–68). Coming from a modest background in Prussia, and largely self-taught, Winckelmann converted to Catholicism in order to pursue his studies in Rome, where he enjoyed the patronage of several prominent cardinals and art lovers. His main work was a *History of Ancient Art* (1764). Goethe, as a student in Leipzig, took classes in drawing from a friend of Winckelmann's, Adam Friedrich Oeser (1717–99), who advocated classicism in art. He hoped to meet, or at least see, Winckelmann when the latter revisited Germany in 1768, but to widespread shock Winckelmann was murdered by a thief during his journey.

Goethe paid a tribute to Winckelmann by writing a biographical essay as a preface to an edition of Winckelmann's letters. He described Winckelmann as by temperament a Greek and a pagan, hence having an intuitive affinity with the ancients and their art, and as a truthful and upright character. He sympathetically acknowledged Winckelmann's homosexuality, remarking that whereas moderns invest their emotions in the relationship between a man and a woman, the Greeks invested theirs in passionate male friendships, and that Winckelmann was a true Greek not least in finding friendship and beauty combined in his relationships with handsome young men. This essay, which must impress us by revealing Goethe's generous tolerance in sexual matters, scandalized contemporaries above all by its evident sympathy for paganism and by thus confirming Goethe's rejection of Christianity.

As this tribute shows, classicism meant for Goethe far more than an artistic style. The Greeks represented for him a way of life that was freer, more spontaneous, closer to the senses, less intellectualized than the modern world. The Greeks cultivated the body equally with the mind; they invented the gymnasium as well as the academy. Hence their art excelled in portraying humanity in its greatest and noblest forms. This of course implied a hopelessly idealized view of the Greeks, ignoring slavery, the oppression of women, genocidal warfare, and the tendency of democracy to become mob rule, but it became an educational orthodoxy in 19th-century Germany.

In Italy, Goethe was surrounded by classical art going back to Greek models. The key moment in his conversion to classicism was his encounter with the classical architecture of Andrea Palladio (1508–80). In Vicenza, where he arrived on 19 September 1786, he was astounded first by Palladio's Teatro Olimpico, then by the Villa Rotonda. The latter, on a hilltop just outside Vicenza, unusually has a classical porch on each of its four sides, from which the occupant can survey all the surrounding countryside, and gains added grandeur from being surmounted by a dome. 'The more one studies Palladio,' wrote Goethe later, 'the more one is staggered by this man's genius, mastery, richness, versatility and grace.' The Palladian style would shape many neoclassical building projects, especially in 18th-century England and America, including Thomas Jefferson's Monticello.

However, Palladio, who relied heavily on the Roman treatise on architecture by Vitruvius, was at several removes from actual Greek buildings. Goethe never visited Greece, but he encountered authentic Greek temples at Paestum in southern Italy. The three massive Doric temples, dating from the 6th century BCE, are nowadays handily close to a railway station, but in Goethe's day one had to make an arduous journey through swamps populated by water-buffalo, and on getting there he felt 'stupefaction' at finding himself 'in a world which was completely strange to me', 'offensive and even terrifying' (*Italian Journey*, 23 March 1787). The huge, chunky temples were so different from the slender columns that Goethe associated with classical architecture that it was over an hour before he could feel reconciled to them.

Another overwhelming experience was Goethe's increasing acquaintance with Raphael, whom he, like many contemporaries, regarded as the supreme Renaissance painter. 'If one encounters a work by Raphael,' he writes after seeing a St Agatha ascribed to him in Bologna (in fact by the Baroque painter Guercino), 'one is at once healed and happy' (*Italian Journey*, 19 October 1786). Raphael exemplified the best relation modern art could have to the Greeks. He did not imitate the Greeks (and could not, since ancient Greek paintings have perished), but he created with the easy mastery that distinguished the Greeks. 'Here', Goethe wrote in 1818, 'we have a talent that sends us fresh water from the primal source. He never imitates the Greeks, but he feels, thinks, acts, just like a Greek.' Goethe concludes: 'Everyone should be a Greek in his own way—but he should be one!'

While in Italy, Goethe was himself diligently drawing and painting, and enjoying the company of living artists. The German artists whom he got to know in Rome and Naples included the internationally famous Angelica Kauffmann (1741–1807), a Swiss painter who had long lived in London and been a founder member of the Royal Academy; the landscape painter Philipp Hackert (1737–1807), whose biography Goethe wrote; and the portraitist Wilhelm Tischbein (1751–1829). Tischbein is famous for his painting *Goethe in the Campagna*, in which Goethe, wearing a white travelling cloak and a broad-brimmed hat, reclines on a rock, with classical ruins in the background (though if you look closely, the artist seems to have given Goethe two left feet). Goethe's interest in art was never that of an antiquarian or a connoisseur; it was always linked to practice and production.

The aesthetics of classicism

Back in Germany, Goethe eventually formed an alliance with Schiller to raise the standard of art and literature, which they thought were in deep decline. They did this through a series of literary journals—Schiller's *Die Horen* (1795–7), Goethe's *Die Propyläen* (1798–1800), and later Goethe's *Über Kunst und Altertum* (*On Art and Antiquity*, 1816–32). It was an uphill struggle: the journals found few subscribers and not enough contributors; Schiller, Goethe, and Goethe's close friend the Swiss art historian Heinrich Meyer (1760–1832), provided much of the copy themselves. Goethe once gloomily compared their campaign to the unsuccessful attempt by the Emperor Julian the Apostate to roll back the triumph of Christianity.

However, Goethe and Schiller, writing against their times, produced not only a body of drama and poetry that has made Weimar classicism into one of the high spots of German literature, but also wide-ranging and profound theories of art. Art theory, or aesthetics, has been a constant preoccupation of German philosophy ever since Alexander Baumgarten originated the term 'aesthetics' in 1750. From Kant and Hegel down to Adorno and Gadamer, most German philosophers have written about art theory. Goethe was perhaps too modest about his philosophical abilities; from his scattered writings, and from his rich correspondence with Schiller, one can make out an aesthetic theory, which can be summarized as follows.

Art imitates nature, but does not copy it. That art reflected nature was an 18th-century commonplace. Goethe's early conviction that art must be true to nature is part of this doctrine, and he retains it, but within a much more ambitious theory. The artist has a duty to depict nature accurately. Hence he must study the anatomy of the human body, as the great Renaissance artists did. But this does not mean that the artist merely *copies* nature. That would be what Goethe and Schiller disapprovingly call 'naturalism'. It is clear that art often pleases us by departing from nature: thus in opera people sing their conversations, which does not happen in real life, but nobody minds.

Art does not copy nature, because art and nature are radically different. Inferior artists aim at the reality of nature, genuine artists aim at the truth of art. One has to realize that artistic truth ('das Kunstwahre') differs entirely from natural truth. For, besides imitating nature, the artist selects and composes: 'the true connoisseur sees not only the truthful imitation, but also the excellent selection, the ingenuity of the composition, the ideal character of the little world of art'. When the artist chooses a natural object to depict, it no longer belongs to nature, for the artist creates it 'since he extracts from it what is significant, characteristic, interesting, or rather confers their higher value on them'. Art does not just imitate the objects we see around us, but shows nature at its best: hence the artist imposes on the human figure 'the more beautiful proportions, the nobler forms, the higher character'.

If art does not imitate the world around us, what does it imitate? Here Goethe is—as he readily admitted—indebted to the aesthetic thought of Karl Philipp Moritz (1756–93), whom he got to know in Rome. Moritz had struggled up from dreadful poverty (described in his autobiographical novel *Anton Reiser*, 1785–90) to become a respected and versatile educator, psychologist, and philosopher. In 1789 Goethe published a sympathetic review of Moritz's treatise *On the Imitation of the Beautiful*, consisting largely of a summary. Moritz's theory of art is basically Neoplatonic: it maintains that all beauty is a reflection of the highest beauty. The highest beauty is embodied in the world as a whole, which is coherent and self-contained. Every beautiful object is a miniature version of the highest beauty, and hence likewise complete in itself. The artist, who has the gift of perceiving beauty, wants not just to perceive it but also to attain it, and the way to attain it is by imitating it. Hence imitation is central to Moritz's theory; but imitation, not of external nature, but of the highest beauty. The artist who intuits the beautiful can form a beautiful object by means of his innate shaping power. Hence Goethe quotes from Moritz the sentence: 'The *born artist* is not satisfied with contemplating nature, he must *imitate* her, *strive after* her.' And what the artist thus produces is a little world in itself, a self-contained object with its own internal coherence.

The work of art shows itself to be coherent and self-contained by its symmetry. It forms a pattern which is not derived from nature but imposed by the artist. And the presence of symmetry explains why even a representation of painful and shocking things can cause aesthetic pleasure. Goethe's example is the *Laocoon*, a sculptural group mentioned by ancient writers and actually dug up in Rome in 1506. It depicts the episode in Virgil's *Aeneid* in which the Trojan priest Laocoon, who has tried to warn his fellow-citizens against the Trojan Horse, is attacked, along with his two sons, by two gigantic snakes emerging from the sea. The Laocoon group was the subject of a famous treatise (1766) by Gotthold Ephraim Lessing (1729–81) and of much further discussion, but while Lessing used it to illustrate what could be depicted in visual art as opposed to writing, Goethe is interested in the aesthetic representation of pain. One of the sons is being encircled by a snake, while the other snake is biting the father in the thigh. The sculptor, according to Goethe, has chosen the moment in the struggle which permits the greatest variety of contrasts and gradations and invites the greatest range of different emotions in the spectator. Thus, despite its painful subject, the Laocoon group is a self-contained, symmetrical, richly patterned and satisfying work of art.

Being a world in itself, the work of art can occasionally go beyond nature. Goethe sometimes expresses this by saying that the artist is also a poet. Thus in the essay 'Ruisdael as Poet' he maintains that the Dutch artist Jacob van Ruisdael (1628/9–82) was not only faithful to nature, but used his poetic imagination to make his landscapes simultaneously real and ideal: 'the artist, feeling purely and thinking clearly, showing himself to be a poet, achieves a perfect symbolism'. In 1827 he discussed with Eckermann a painting by Peter Paul Rubens (1577–1640), *Return from the Fields*, in which close inspection reveals that the light is falling in two different directions. Goethe justifies this contradiction as being 'higher than nature'. Of course the artist must depict nature faithfully: for example, he must not change the anatomy of an animal. 'But in the higher regions of artistic activity, when a picture becomes an independent image, he has freer play, and here he may have recourse to *fictions*, as Rubens has done with the double lighting in his landscape' (to Eckermann, 18 April 1827). The great artist can show his creative individuality in his work.

At its greatest, art *is* nature. Although the two are distinct, in classical art they coincide. Great art has the inevitability that natural objects have: it *has* to be the way it is. 'These masterpieces of man were brought forth in obedience to the same laws as the masterpieces of nature. Before them, all that is arbitrary and imaginary collapses: *there* is Necessity, *there* is God' (*Italian Journey*, 5 September 1787). After seeing Raphael's *Transfiguration* in a Roman convent, Goethe is convinced that 'like nature, Raphael is always right, and most profoundly so when we understand him least' (*Italian Journey*, December 1787).

These theoretical reflections are always prompted by specific works of art, and can be checked against the experience of art. In the introduction to the first issue of his journal, *Die Propyläen*, Goethe, having set out his views, adds that all the maxims about art he has expressed must be put to a practical test. It is almost impossible to reach agreement on theoretical principles, but one can very quickly find out what works or doesn't work. Not surprisingly, Goethe excels in art appreciation. Scattered through his writings and conversations are many sensitive, lovingly detailed descriptions of such paintings as Leonardo's *Last Supper*, Andrea Mantegna's *Triumph of Caesar*, and works by Rembrandt, Claude Lorrain, Caspar David Friedrich, and Eugène Delacroix. Nor is it surprising that Goethe enthusiastically collected art, including plaster casts of famous sculptures and copies of paintings. His collection contains over 26,500 items, comprising drawings, paintings, coins, gems, medals, sculptures, porcelain, and much else. A selection is nowadays displayed to the public in Goethe's house on the Frauenplan in Weimar (see Figure 6).

6. Goethe's house on the Frauenplan in Weimar.

Classicism or Romanticism?

By now the reader may be surprised to find Goethe so firmly associated with Classicism. Literary histories written in English sometimes assign him to the Romantic movement; *Werther* often ranks among the founding texts of Romanticism; and the story of the eternally unsatisfied Faust seems an archetypally Romantic narrative.

However, there is no contradiction here. Period terms such as Romanticism are simply a convenient way for historians to arrange writers in groups. They do not express any actual *Zeitgeist* or 'spirit of the age'; they are at best a necessary over-simplification of the complex facts of history; and they do not always correspond to how writers thought of themselves. None of the British 'Romantic' poets from Wordsworth to Byron called himself a Romantic, whereas the term was used by the writers, centring on the Schlegel brothers, who were active in Jena (near Goethe's Weimar) from about 1800 onwards. German literary historians use the term 'Sturm und Drang' for an earlier phase (often seen as anticipating Romanticism) when young writers, including Goethe, challenged literary and social convention, exalted passion above reason, wrote realist dramas in supposedly Shakespearean form, admired folk poetry, and advocated a popular German art as against a courtly art based on French neoclassical models. *Werther*, which exalts passion (but also warns against its excesses), belongs to this period.

The 'Sturm und Drang' Goethe was also an enthusiast for Shakespeare. In 1771 he gave a lecture on Shakespeare's name-day, 14 October, praising him as the poet of nature, in contrast to the artificial drama of France. His early play *Götz von Berlichingen*, inspired by Shakespeare's history plays, gives a broad picture of early 16th-century Germany, stretching over several decades and with innumerable changes of scene; horsemen ride across the stage, a castle is besieged, a soldier drowns in a swamp. The play was influential: not only did it initiate a German fashion for dramas and tales about medieval knights, but it was translated into English (very inaccurately) by Walter Scott and showed how a panorama of a past era might be presented in fiction, as Scott would do in *Ivanhoe* and many other historical novels.

For the young Goethe, poetry was the voice of the people. Encouraged by his friend, the clergyman and critic Johann Gottfried Herder (1744–1803), whom he met in Strasbourg and for whom in 1776 he would procure a position in Weimar, Goethe collected folk-songs among the German-speaking farmers of Alsace, and himself wrote poems in popular styles such as 'Heidenröslein' (later set to music by Schubert and others). Sharing the general enthusiasm for James Macpherson's 'Ossian', Goethe obtained the English text, studied the specimens of Gaelic which Macpherson had appended to it, and made his own translation of them. When he encountered a Serbian ballad with a German translation, he made his own version, using the Serbian text to get a sense of the rhythm; the result, 'Lament of the Noble Wives of Azan Aga', was included by Herder in his collection of folk-songs from around the world.

When the German Romantics came on the scene, Goethe was reserved. He and Schiller regarded the Schlegel brothers primarily as critics, occasionally profound but often uninteresting and sometimes spiteful. In the late 1790s Goethe was intent on a study of Homer, and on working out the structural features which distinguished epic from drama. The Romantics, by contrast, were exploring medieval art and literature, with an increasing interest in the Catholic religiosity that underpinned them. Goethe was broad-minded enough to acknowledge the good qualities of many Romantic writers and painters, and from 1810 was a close friend of the art historian Sulpiz Boisserée who helped to revive interest in Gothic architecture. Nevertheless, he could not stand the 'neo-Catholic sentimentalism' that so many Romantics promoted, and the tales of terror by Romantic writers such as E. T. A. Hoffmann (1776–1822) struck him as pathological and repellent. It remains surprising that while he was writing *Elective Affinities* in 1808–9 Goethe had as a house guest the Romantic playwright Zacharias Werner, an erratic character who soon afterwards converted to Catholicism and ended up as a fashionable preacher in Vienna; the supernatural suggestions in the novel have been ascribed to Werner's influence. Goethe's last word on the subject is reported by Eckermann (2 April 1829):

> I call the classical that which is healthy, and the romantic that which is sick. And the *Nibelungenlied* [the German medieval epic] is as classical as Homer, for both are healthy and sound. Most modern work is romantic, not because it is new, but because it is feeble, sickly and sick, and the ancient is classical, not because it is old, but because it is strong, fresh, happy and healthy. If we distinguish the classical and the romantic by such qualities, we shall soon be clear in our minds.

Classicism, for Goethe, was no mere theory. It had to issue in literary creation. As a dramatist, he turned his back on the Shakespearean form of *Götz* and adopted classical form for his plays *Iphigenie in Tauris* (completed in Italy, 1786–7) and *Torquato Tasso* (1790—both to be discussed in future chapters). But this did not mean returning to Greek drama. With their five-act structure, stylized blank-verse dialogue, small cast, and intense concentration achieved by strictly observing the unities of time and place, these plays follow the rules of drama prescribed by neoclassical critics almost as closely as the dramas of Jean Racine a century earlier. And, as with Racine, they use classical concentration to achieve dramatic tension and rich psychological subtlety.

Similarly, Goethe's studies of Homer made him want to write a Homeric epic. But his attempt at an epic poem on the death of Achilles, the *Achilleis* (1799), faltered after one—admittedly impressive—canto. He had far greater success with *Hermann und Dorothea* (1797), where German small-town life is depicted in Homeric verse which provides both epic dignity and humorous irony. Goethe realized that one could not simply recreate classical literature: in adopting classical forms, one had ironically to acknowledge one's own modernity and hence one's distance from the ancient world.

World literature

Goethe's curiosity about literature always extended well beyond Germany. Late in life he uttered the famous dictum: 'National literature no longer means much, the age of world literature is at hand' (to Eckermann, 31 January 1827). He continued to believe that ancient Greek literature represented an absolute standard. But he was anxious to appreciate what was excellent in every accessible literature. For this purpose, Goethe even around the age of 80 still kept up with contemporary literature in French, Italian, and English, reading literary reviews from various countries to inform himself. He valued highly the work of cultural intermediaries such as Thomas Carlyle (1795–1881), who translated *Wilhelm Meister's Apprenticeship* into English, along with many German Romantic texts, and wrote a biography of Schiller. The two had a cordial correspondence; Goethe even wrote Carlyle a reference when the latter applied unsuccessfully for the Chair of Moral Philosophy at St Andrews.

Goethe's literary tastes were wide-ranging but not omnivorous. When in Italy he enjoyed annoying the Italians by disparaging their national poet, Dante: 'I had never been able to understand how people could take the trouble to read these poems. I thought the *Inferno* absolutely horrible, the *Purgatorio* ambiguous, and the *Paradiso* boring' (*Italian Journey*, July 1787). His early enthusiasm for Shakespeare was qualified by his belief—common at that time—that Shakespeare's plays were better read than performed. As director of the Weimar Court Theatre, therefore, Goethe paid less attention to Shakespeare than to the Spanish dramatist Pedro Calderón de la Barca (1600–81), whose highly visual theatrical style reconciled Goethe even to the intensely Catholic character of his plays. Among contemporary writers, Goethe shared the Europe-wide enthusiasm for Byron, but the great discovery of his later years was Alessandro Manzoni, particularly Manzoni's historical novel *The Betrothed* (1827), which, he said, 'surpasses everything we know in this genre' (to Eckermann, 18 July 1827)—hence, by implication, was better than the hugely popular historical novels by Scott. With younger German writers, Goethe's judgement was less sure. He has often been blamed for disparaging works by Friedrich Hölderlin (1770–1844) and Heinrich von Kleist (1778–1811) whom posterity has placed among the leading writers of their age; but the poems Hölderlin showed him were minor work, while his refusal to stage Kleist's *Penthesilea* is more than understandable, since this great but shocking tragedy, in which unhappy love culminates in cannibalism, could only be appreciated against the background of the 20th-century theatre of cruelty.

Goethe's reading extended to the literatures of Asia, which were becoming available through translations, especially by the great philologist Sir William Jones, whom Goethe called 'the incomparable Jones', and who translated from Arabic, Persian, and Sanskrit. Goethe shared the general enthusiasm especially for the Sanskrit play *Sakontala* (by Kālidāsa, *c.*400 CE), which had been translated into English by Jones and thence into German by Georg Forster. He wrote a quatrain in praise of this play's immense charm. Late in life we find Goethe telling Eckermann that he has been reading and enjoying a Chinese novel (31 January 1827); this appears to have been a 17th-century romance entitled, in the English version Goethe used, *Chinese Courtship in Verse*, but he seems to have read at least two other Chinese novels in English or French translations. These translations were important, not only because they made unknown masterpieces available in Europe, but because they combated Eurocentrism by revealing the richness of the ancient cultures of the Middle and Far East.

With his hands-on approach, Goethe could not read foreign literatures without a creative response, which often took the form of translations. He translated directly from French, Italian, and English (including the first five stanzas of Byron's *Don Juan*), and from French versions of modern Greek heroic ballads and South American songs. He made his own versions of Middle Eastern texts—extracts from the Koran, the pre-Islamic poems known as the *Mu'allaqat*, the Song of Solomon from the Old Testament—by drawing on Latin, German, and increasingly English translations. Translation became creative adaptation when in 1828 Goethe published, as 'Chinese–German Seasons and Times of Day', fourteen short poems inspired by Chinese models.

Although most of Goethe's translations are short, he deserves credit as a cultural mediator for two major achievements. He translated in 1803 the autobiography of the Italian Renaissance goldsmith Benvenuto Cellini (1500–71) and soon afterwards the satirical novel in dialogue, *Le Neveu de Rameau* (*Rameau's Nephew*) by Denis Diderot (1713–84). The manuscript of the latter, unpublished during Diderot's lifetime, found its way by a roundabout route to Schiller, who persuaded Goethe to translate it in 1804–5. Both texts focus on talented misfits: Cellini is constantly falling out with his employer, the Pope, who values his abilities but finds him an impossible person; the Nephew refuses to compromise with conventional society and relentlessly attacks its beliefs. Did these translations enable Goethe, a mainstay of courtly society who defied its conventions by his relationship with Christiane Vulpius, to express his other, anti-social self?

The *West-Eastern Divan*

The delighted exploration of a foreign culture, and the liberating exploration of an alternative self, are undertaken in the great collection of Orientalizing poetry that Goethe published in 1819. In 1814 he read the translation made by the Austrian diplomat Joseph von Hammer-Purgstall of the *Divan* by the 14th-century poet Hafiz. This prompted Goethe to seek further translations from Persian and Arabic literature and find out all he could about it, then to write his own poems.

From Hammer-Purgstall's introduction, Goethe learnt that Muhammad Shemseddin, known as Hafiz because he had learnt the Koran by heart, lived all his life in the Persian city of Shiraz; that he belonged to an order of Sufi mystics; that he charged his co-religionists with hypocrisy because they disapproved of his hedonistic poems about wine and love; that he enjoyed the protection of successive princes; and that when Timur (Tamerlane, 1336–1405) conquered Persia, he sent for the then elderly Hafiz, praised him, and treated him kindly. Parallels between Hafiz and Goethe were numerous: Goethe had lived for almost forty years, with just one break, in Weimar, supported by a prince; he was attacked by the religious; and, like Hafiz, he lived in an age of upheaval which had been going on since 1789. So in one sense the *Divan* represents Goethe's flight from modern Europe, increasingly dominated by warfare and nationalism, into the older civilization of the Orient. Hence the opening poem is called 'Hegire', after Muhammad's flight (*hejira*) from Mecca to Medina in the founding year of the Muslim calendar. But in other ways the world of Hafiz recreates Goethe's. Timur features in several poems, and others refer pointedly to 'tyrants' and 'conquerors', keeping us in mind of Napoleon, who in 1808 had summoned Goethe to meet him as Timur did Hafiz.

Although Goethe found in Hafiz a kindred spirit, he does not identify with him. Nor does he 'appropriate' the Orient, professing knowledge of it and hence virtual power over it, as Western writers on Asia have in recent decades been charged with doing. Rather, he explores the Middle East, feeling his way into it and suggesting analogies with his own world. Thus the poetic voice of the *Divan* conducts an imaginary interview with Hafiz, asking the meaning of his name, and remarking that he too, however sceptical, is deeply impregnated with his own holy scripture. Some of Hafiz's traits are ascribed to the persona of Hatem, the elderly, white-haired man who feels rejuvenated by his love for Zuleika. Hafiz's tense relationship with the Islamic authorities provides another affinity: Goethe doubts his supposed mysticism and portrays him as a hedonist, enjoying himself with wine, women, and his handsome young cupbearer. In conversation Goethe referred to Hafiz as 'a second Voltaire'.

The religious authorities are often present. Goethe versifies an actual *fatwa*, reported by Hammer-Purgstall, which diplomatically concluded that Hafiz's poems, though mostly commendable, contained 'some trifles beyond the boundaries of the law'. The Hafiz of the poems is happy in the earthly world without being devout, and hopes that the poet's eloquence will gain him access to Paradise. Meanwhile, Goethe subtly undermines the authority of Islam (with Christianity in mind) by introducing the legends and fairy-tales of which Muhammad, according to Goethe's explanatory notes, disapproved. We hear of Chiser, the green-clad nature-spirit who makes the earth fertile, and of the four women and four animals who have been admitted to Paradise. Goethe also celebrates the nature-worship of the ancient Persians, who venerated the sun, and inserts many significant allusions to the sun and fire, thus subtly undermining later theological systems. The famous poem about death and rebirth, 'Selige Sehnsucht' (Blessed Yearning), differs from both Christianity and Islam in hinting at a transmigration of the soul through fire to a higher form of being.

The physical world of the poems is sensuous and luxurious. Against the background of the desert, traversed by merchants' caravans from 'Hindustan' to the Red Sea, and from Bukhara to Arabia, we imagine cities with bazaars, baths, and taverns, and luxurious palaces where an avenue lined by cypresses leads to a fountain. The hoopoe (which according to the Koran bore a message from the Queen of Sheba to Solomon) may cross one's path, the bulbul (Persian nightingale) sings in the garden, where roses and lilies grow. Jewels, spices, and perfumes—ambergris, musk, attar of roses—complete the atmosphere of luxury. Altogether the *Divan* is a veiled protest against the Christian tradition of disparaging the physical, earthly world in favour of an unknown spiritual realm.

Being 'west-eastern', the *Divan* contains many anachronistic, playful allusions to Western culture. In one poem, quoted here to illustrate the simplicity and concision Goethe attains, classicism is invoked, set against its opposite, and the two reconciled in a higher synthesis:

Lied und Gebilde

Mag der Grieche seinen Thon
Zu Gestalten drücken
An der eignen Hände Sohn
Steigern sein Entzücken;

Aber uns ist wonnereich
In den Euphrat greifen,
Und im flüssgen Element
Hin und wider schweifen.

Löscht ich so der Seele Brand
Lied es wird erschallen;
Schöpft des Dichters reine Hand
Wasser wird sich ballen.

Song and Form

Let the Greek mould his clay into shapes and take ever-increasing delight in the son of his own hands. || But to us it is bliss to dip our fingers into the Euphrates and to drift to and fro in the liquid element. || When I have thus quenched my soul's fire, my song shall sound forth; when the poet's pure hand draws water, the water will become a ball.

Greek art is typified by the limited, self-contained, visible, and tangible statue. Oriental art (like Romanticism) is close to nature, fluid, and boundless. But once the poet has transmuted his turbulent emotions (we remember the 'heart on fire' of 'To the Moon'), the poem, however fluid its materials, will take shape as though by itself, in response to the poet's invitation. Goethe's German contains a discreet pun on *schöpfen* ('to draw water') and *Schöpfer* ('creator'). Poetic creation, transcending the conflict between Classicism and Romanticism, is identified with the archetypal human action of drawing water. As in Goethe's aesthetic theory, art, at its supreme point, becomes identical with nature.

Chapter 4
Politics

The Holy Roman Empire

In Goethe's lifetime, and until the creation of the Second German Empire in 1871, there was no country called Germany. Most of the German-speaking lands belonged nominally to the Holy Roman Empire, a loose confederation of states dating back to the early Middle Ages. The Emperor was supposedly elected by seven German princes who had the title of Elector, but in practice the office of Emperor had been hereditary in the Habsburg family since 1438; Goethe witnessed, and described in his autobiography, the coronation of Joseph II as Emperor in Frankfurt in 1765. The Emperor ruled his own domain, Austria, but had no real power over the 300 or so other territories comprising the Empire. These included some important states (Austria, Prussia, Saxony, Bavaria), about 100 smaller states ruled by secular princes or princes of the Church (such as the Archbishop of Salzburg), many even smaller units which were really noblemen's estates, and 51 self-governing cities of which Goethe's native Frankfurt was among the largest.

The Empire was widely considered an anachronism. The Imperial Diet (*Reichstag*) took no decisions: it consisted only of envoys from the various princes, who delivered prepared speeches. The princes themselves never agreed on a common policy. There was a Supreme Court (*Reichskammergericht*), located in the tiny independent city of Wetzlar (population 5,000), near Frankfurt, to which the young lawyer Goethe was attached from May to September 1772; he describes in his autobiography how under-resourced, understaffed, and ineffectual it was. In 1772 there were 61,233 cases still undecided. When Napoleon, having invaded Germany, formally dissolved the Empire on 6 August 1806, nobody much noticed. Goethe, travelling by coach from Carlsbad to Weimar, recorded in his diary for 7 August: 'Quarrel between the servant and the coachman on the box, which excited us more than the break-up of the Empire.'

However, the mode of princely government under the Empire permanently shaped Goethe's conception of politics. German princes, whatever the size of their territories, were absolute rulers, in sharp contrast to the constitutional monarchs of Britain. In Germany there were very few parliaments or other representative institutions that could curtail a prince's powers. The most one could hope for was that a prince would take his responsibilities seriously and exercise what historians have since called 'enlightened absolutism'. This did often happen. Frederick the Great, who as King of Prussia from 1740 to 1786 made his bleak and infertile country into a major European power, declared on assuming power that the sovereign should not be the absolute master of his people, but their first servant, and devoted himself whole-heartedly to efficient government. Many others followed his example, helped and often impelled by the large body of university-trained bureaucrats who were needed to administer every state and who were usually keen to introduce practical reforms, such as improving roads, providing for the poor, and introducing better farming methods.

One such bureaucrat especially shaped Goethe's political ideals. Justus Möser, chief administrator of the small principality of Osnabrück in north-western Germany, published newspaper articles, collected as *Patriotic Musings*, on questions of domestic management, economy, and government. Besides deploring young women's over-expenditure on clothes, advising on the treatment of beggars, and discussing the decline in rural commerce, Möser addresses large questions of administration. He opposes a one-size-fits-all policy that would standardize legal provisions and rights throughout Germany. Instead, he advocates respect for local traditions and praises diversity for its own sake. Writing about German history, he looks back to a remote golden age when landowners were directly subject to the Emperor and regrets the subsequent rise of powerful princes. He shares the widespread view that just as the father is the head of the household, so the prince should be the father of his people (*Landesvater*), exercising benevolent patriarchal authority.

All this pleased Goethe. He valued the local traditions of Frankfurt, of which his maternal grandfather had been *Schultheiss* or chief official (though his father took no part in local government). He liked what was particular and individual, and disliked abstraction in politics as elsewhere. He happily accepted the traditional hierarchical organization of German society into *Stände* or ranks, with the nobility at the top, then *Bürger* or non-noble elites ('bourgeois' would be a misleading translation), then craftsmen and artisans, then the agricultural workers who formed well over half of the Empire's population. (In the 18th century there were only the beginnings of an industrial proletariat.) He professed to believe that the aristocracy was established by God. In his literary works he often criticizes social mobility. Thus in *Hermann and Dorothea* (1797), with gentle humour but serious intent, he praises the traditional life of a small German town; the hero Hermann resolves to remain in his station in life as innkeeper, despite his father's aspirations for him. By contrast, an upstart businessman unkindly joins his daughters in mocking Hermann for not knowing the latest songs from *The Magic Flute*—the kind of fashionable affectation that Möser criticized. So we must understand Goethe's political outlook as deeply conservative.

Goethe's conservatism was not typical of his time. Many contemporary German intellectuals deplored princely power and wanted human rights to be safeguarded. Schiller gave a scathing picture of oppression and intrigue in a petty court in his play *Kabale und Liebe* (*Intrigue and Love*, 1784); contemplated emigrating to America if the revolution there were successful; denounced political and clerical tyranny in *Don Carlos* (1787); and wrote to Goethe: 'When I meet a prince, I always wonder if he is good for anything' (letter, 29 January 1795). Kant's famous essay 'An Answer to the Question: What is Enlightenment?' (1784) urged people to free themselves from intellectual immaturity (*Unmündigkeit*) and learn to think independently. Goethe did think independently; and his independent thinking led him to a principled conservatism.

Weimar

But Goethe's conservatism was complicated and individual. Although he disapproved of social mobility, he was himself upwardly mobile in accepting in 1775 an invitation from the young Duke of Weimar to join his court. In 1782 Goethe was raised to the nobility, which entitled him to insert 'von' in his name and to dine at the Duke's table. Yet from 1788, as we have seen, he defied all social conventions by living with a lower-class woman. His decision testifies not only to the attraction of Christiane Vulpius but also to his deep discomfort with the shallowness and hypocrisy of court life.

Carl August (1757–1828), eight years younger than Goethe, succeeded to the Duchy in September 1775. He made a dynastic marriage, which proved unhappy, and for which he compensated with love-affairs and eventually by keeping a recognized mistress. He was intelligent but not intellectual, fond of theatre, opera, sport, and soldiering, anxious to rule his principality responsibly. The town of Weimar, with 6,000 inhabitants, was the centre of the petty principality of Saxe-Weimar-Eisenach, which consisted of two separate territories, with a population of some 106,000 and an area of about 700 square miles. Most of the inhabitants were peasants, living often in miserable conditions, and supporting by their taxes the traditional extravagant life-style of a princely court. Not only did peasants have to till their lord's fields as well as their own, but their own crops were often ruined by noble huntsmen pursuing the quarry heedlessly through cornfields. Goethe knew what their lives were like. 'I see the peasant scraping a meagre living from the soil which could support him comfortably if he worked only for himself,' he wrote to his friend Knebel, 'but you know that when the aphids on rose-petals have sucked themselves fat and green, the ants come along and suck the juice out of their bodies' (17 April 1782). Here, albeit indirectly, he denounces the aristocracy as parasites.

Although the famous author of *Werther* had initially been recruited simply as an interesting companion for the Duke, within six months of his arrival he was given the title of Legation Councillor (*Legationsrat*) and appointed to the four-man Privy Council which governed the duchy. A 26-year-old lawyer with no administrative experience was an eccentric choice. Yet Goethe justified it. Besides attending Council meetings two or three mornings a week, and helping to decide issues ranging from foreign policy to digging a well, he undertook, with acknowledged efficiency, a series of responsibilities: for mining, road-building, maintaining the army, and finance. Weimar's finances were a particular headache. The duchy lived far beyond its income. It had few natural resources—hence the desperate and ultimately futile efforts to reopen the silver mine at Ilmenau—and no industry apart from stocking-making, a cottage industry that was in severe decline because of foreign competition. Goethe did his best. The Duke's favourite extravagance was his army of 500 men, whom he loved to drill. The threat of state bankruptcy enabled Goethe to get it reduced to 136 men. Otherwise, however, Weimar was a stagnating economy in which there seemed no alternative to exploiting the rural population.

Recent research has shown that Goethe thoroughly supported the conservative policies in force at Weimar. The peasants sent in petitions protesting against the unlawful extension of their labour services, which were supposed to be limited by ancient statute, but the Privy Council rejected their pleas and punished them for protesting. In 1783, when the Duke asked the Privy Council to consider abolishing the death penalty for infanticide, Goethe, opposing the Duke's evident preference, voted successfully for keeping it. The immediate result was the execution of a young woman, Johanna Höhn. The Duke left town to avoid witnessing it; so did the Weimar intellectual Bode, who described it as 'state murder'. This is the more noteworthy since the law which condemned the unmarried mother to a cruel penalty, yet did not pursue the father, had been denounced by intellectuals throughout the 1770s. Goethe, who, despite his comparative youth, exerted decisive influence as the Duke's closest friend, could have saved Höhn's life, but did not. German intellectuals have often longed to be close to power; Goethe did have power (albeit in a tiny state), but did not use it as one might have wished him to.

The French Revolution

For Goethe, the French Revolution was 'the most dreadful of all events'. The fall of the Bastille on 14 July 1789 set off a series of upheavals which affected all of Europe and came at least to a symbolic end with Napoleon's final defeat at Waterloo in 1815. At first, the radical reforms in France were welcomed by many German intellectuals. The French National Assembly issued the Declaration of the Rights of Man and the Citizen in August 1789, nationalized the property of the Church, formally abolished the nobility, and eventually, since the King tried to resist these measures, deposed, imprisoned, and executed him. A Prussian army, supported by French émigrés and by other German states including Weimar, invaded France in August 1792, hoping to roll back the Revolution. Goethe, reluctantly accompanying the Weimar contingent, witnessed the battle of Valmy on 20

September, and experienced the horrors of the subsequent retreat. He was also present at the siege of Mainz, where local revolutionaries, helped by French troops, had installed a radical government that most of the population rejected.

By his own account, Goethe said at Valmy: 'Here begins a new epoch of world history', meaning presumably that the new phenomenon of a citizen army had defeated the mercenary troops of the old régime. But if Goethe really said this, it must have been with foreboding. In Robespierre's Reign of Terror (1793–4), which can be attributed both to the internal dynamics of the Revolution and to the panic caused by foreign invasion, some 17,000 people were executed by the guillotine or otherwise, and one in ten of the adult French population spent time in prison. After Robespierre and his associates had themselves been guillotined, the government of France passed to the five-man Directory and then in 1799 to the military despot Napoleon. Napoleon divided his energies between internal reforms and foreign conquests. On 14 October 1806 he broke the military power of Prussia at the battle of Jena, only a few miles from Weimar. French troops occupied the town. They burst into Goethe's house, demanding food and wine; intimidated by Goethe's dignified appearance even in his dressing-gown, they withdrew, but then returned and entered his bedroom with fixed bayonets; the resourceful Christiane raised the alarm and fetched men to drive them out. Most of Germany remained under Napoleon's control until his defeat in Russia in the winter of 1812–13.

While Goethe found the Revolution and its consequences appalling, he also thought that the French aristocracy had brought their fate on themselves. He was profoundly disturbed by the Diamond Necklace affair, a swindle carried out by a daring adventuress upon an aristocratic Cardinal and Marie-Antoinette herself, and dramatized it in *Der Groß-Cophta* (*The Grand Cophta*, 1791), one of several more or less farcical plays in which he responded to the Revolution. Here Goethe shows little awareness that popular resentment against misrule might have propelled the Revolution. His plays, mostly set in small-town Germany, feature gullible peasants, malevolent would-be politicians, and aristocrats who intervene to restore order. The message is clear: ordinary people should mind their own business; agitators are evil and self-seeking; politics are the concern only of the governing class, who need to exercise their responsibility properly.

A much finer work, though still with a clear message, is *Hermann und Dorothea* (1797). Dorothea is a German refugee, driven from the left bank of the Rhine by revolutionary troops; Hermann (as we have seen) a young German who upholds the solid, independent traditions of middle-class life. The refugees include a wise Judge who admits that the promises of the Revolution were at first seductive. The apparent dawn of freedom, the proclamation of the rights of man, stirred people's hearts and seemed to herald an end to misgovernment by idle and selfish elites. But this enthusiasm was short-lived. The revolutionary armies were not liberators but brutal oppressors. Dorothea's previous fiancé, an idealistic young man, went to Paris and perished by the guillotine. Hermann concludes that Germans should not dream of revolution but protect what they have. The alliance between him and Dorothea is the centre round which are arranged the household, the wider family, the town, and the (cultural) German nation.

The Revolution therefore seemed to show how justified Goethe's conservatism was. If ordinary people meddled in politics, the result could only be disaster, anarchy, and destruction. The Revolution confirmed the fears of many 18th-century thinkers that a republican government would be torn apart by hostile parties or factions. Hence, although it was first and foremost the French monarchy and aristocracy who had ruined their country through misgovernment, Goethe never thought that the answer might be to involve more people in government through representative institutions. The answer to bad aristocracy was good aristocracy, and—ideally—an alliance between the good aristocracy and the middle classes, as symbolized by the cross-class marriages at the end of *Wilhelm Meister's Apprenticeship*.

The traumatic effects of the Revolution and its aftermath explain why Goethe set so much store by order. A well-known statement from his account of the siege of Mainz has often been held against him: 'In the end I said impatiently: "that's just how I am, I would rather commit an injustice than put up with disorder."' But if we know the context, things look different. After the city, held by revolutionaries, had fallen to the German troops that Goethe was accompanying, suspected *Clubbisten* (members of the Jacobin Club) were often beaten up by the vindictive populace. Goethe tells how he saw a man on horseback, accompanied by a woman, being threatened by the crowd. Realizing how tense the situation was, Goethe cried: 'Stop!' The crowd drew back; Goethe told them firmly that no violence was permitted in the Duke of Weimar's camp. Despite grumbling from the crowd, the man and woman made their escape, having thanked Goethe for probably saving their lives. A friend reproached Goethe for his foolhardy intervention in a dangerous situation; whereupon Goethe made his famous reply. He had committed an injustice, since the man was a well-known revolutionary who merited punishment; but it was better to let him go than to allow the crowd to practise lynch law. Even if the story is not actually true (no independent corroboration has been found), it serves as an exemplary anecdote illustrating an important principle.

With the passage of time, Goethe's conservatism hardened. He disapproved of the freedom of the press, because it allowed irresponsible people to pass opinions on politics. When the Jena scientist Lorenz Oken commented on politics in his journal *Isis* in 1816, Goethe wrote an official report denouncing Oken in almost hysterical terms; Oken was told to choose between his journal and his Jena chair, and chose the former, moving to a post at Munich. Goethe was hostile to the whole conception of a public sphere in which democratic debate could be conducted. He deplored also the formation of political parties, which he thought wasted energy and encouraged hatred. When the Duke in 1823 issued an ordinance allowing Jews to practise their religion, marry non-Jews, and attend schools and universities, Goethe deplored this 'scandalous law' which would 'undermine all moral feelings in families'. The radicals of the 1830s who dismissed Goethe as a 'Fürstenknecht' (slave to a prince) were wrong: here again, as in the debate on punishing infanticide, Goethe was *more* conservative than his prince.

Politics in literature

Yet when we turn to Goethe's literary works—apart from the highly ideological texts inspired directly by the French Revolution—we find that their treatment of political issues is complex and ambivalent, and that it sometimes contradicts or undermines the principles Goethe upheld as a servant of his ducal employer. His practical inclinations led in one direction, his imagination in another. The most glaring example is the tragedy of Gretchen in *Faust I* (based partly on the actual fate of the infanticide Susanne Margarete Brandt in Goethe's Frankfurt in 1772). For committing infanticide when abandoned by her lover Faust, she suffers the very penalty that Goethe as a member of the Privy Council had refused to soften.

Goethe's literary works repeatedly visit those difficult areas which as a citizen he did his best to disregard. As we have seen, he was deeply attached to the hierarchical, feudal order which was looking shaky even before the French Revolution. But several of his historical dramas are set in the transition from feudalism to a later, and not clearly better, state of society.

In *Götz von Berlichingen* (1773) Goethe vividly brought to life German society in the early 16th century. The hero Götz is a knight, deeply attached, in the spirit of Justus Möser, to his local area, and owing allegiance directly to the Emperor. But times are changing; a uniform system of Roman law is replacing local jurisdictions; old German customs are yielding to new fashions acquired in Italy; and small landowners like Götz are coming under the power of princes who rule large territories. Götz's former friend Weislingen, a smooth and adaptable courtier, has chosen to make his career in the new order. He rises rapidly, becomes a confidant of the Emperor, and uses his position to persecute Götz with a fury based on envy of Götz's superior character. And Götz is vulnerable, because he lives partly by highway robbery, and knights like him are a pest in the new world that is being unified by commerce. The play presents Götz, who dies uttering the word 'Freedom!', in the most attractive light, but cannot conceal that people like him are an anachronism. Yet a world where Weislingen can succeed is hardly better.

Goethe returned to the 16th century in *Egmont* (completed in 1788). It is 1566. We are in the Netherlands, ruled from Catholic Spain, but increasingly inclined towards Protestantism. Proponents of the new religion have wrecked churches and destroyed religious images. Spanish troops led by the Duke of Alba are expected to arrive and suppress these disorders brutally. Count Egmont, based on the historical statesman (1522–68), is a popular leader and war hero, who regards the Emperor—now Philip II of Spain—as his feudal superior and naively expects fair treatment from him. His fellow-statesman and temperamental opposite, Oranien, rightly foresees an invasion and flees abroad to organize resistance, while Egmont stays and is treacherously imprisoned. For Egmont, politics are about love and loyalty, while Oranien regards them as a game of chess. Oranien's calculations are unattractive, yet he is proved right; moreover, Oranien is the person known to history as William of Orange (1533–84), who successfully led the Dutch revolt against Spanish rule. The play reveals nothing about Oranien's future, but tells us that Egmont's execution will inspire the Dutch to fight for freedom. So Goethe claims our sympathies for the attractive but naive and doomed hero, and diverts them away from the shrewd and successful politician.

Several scenes show the ordinary citizens, some of whom have fought under Egmont's command. They also include the agitator Vansen, a scribe, hence a relatively educated person, who tells the Dutch about their ancient rights recorded in documents which he has seen. There is no reason to disbelieve him, yet everyone dislikes Vansen and describes him as a bad character. The play invites us to consider Vansen a malicious trouble-maker, a barrack-room lawyer, who merely foments disorder. Yet the Dutch people do have traditional rights and should not be dependent on the whim of their superiors.

As in *Götz*, the word 'freedom' is much used. In the confrontation between Alba and Egmont, Alba declares that a well-behaved citizen has as much freedom as he needs: 'What is the freest man free to do? What is right! And the King will not prevent him from doing that.' This denies any right to participation in politics. Yet earlier in the play, quelling a tumult, Egmont has said something very similar: 'A good citizen earning his living by honest work will always enjoy all the liberty he needs.' And Goethe himself, in old age, expressed a similar view: 'If anyone has the freedom to lead a healthy life and do his job, then he has enough, and anyone can easily have that much' (to Eckermann, 18 January 1827). Goethe shares the common 18th-century view that security under the law is the best kind of freedom, and that the widening of participation in politics brings dangerous instability.

'Freedom' also means freedom from foreign rule. But the play says little about how to resist oppression. Oranien's resistance lies in the future, and beyond what the play can express. Nor has Egmont any solution to the problem of religious conflict: he simply tells people to 'stand firm in the true faith', which they plainly are not doing and, as we know from history, did not do. Goethe shows that feudalism has had its day, and exposes its ineffectuality, but he sees nothing positive in the political pragmatism which is replacing it.

While *Egmont* was written before the French Revolution, Goethe responded to the Revolution not only in his ideological dramas but later in his enigmatic play *Die natürliche Tochter* (*The Natural Daughter*, 1803). The setting is an unnamed kingdom, suggesting France, whose King feels unable to cope with the political upheavals he foresees. Eugenie (meaning 'well-born'), the illegitimate daughter of a Duke, embodies feudal loyalty. She insists on kneeling before the King. When he remonstrates, she replies in words that beautifully convey what feudalism at its best *may* have been:

> The feeling that compels us to our knees,
> In rapturous moments, is delightful too.
> This is the posture that can best express
> The purest sacrifice we long to make
> Unto our king, our father, and our God,
> In blissful gratitude and boundless love. (lines 350–5)

Alas, the selfless Eugenie finds herself enmeshed in cynical intrigues. Her father and brother, assisted by the Secretary, want her banished to the West Indies, so that her inevitable death from fever will release her inheritance. The Secretary embodies selfish calculation, the antithesis of feudal loyalty. He states his belief:

> Our intellect was given us so that,
> Being mature, we can survive on earth.
> What serves our interests is our highest law. (lines 859–61)

'Mature' here translates *mündig*, 'of age', the word that for Kant typified humanity's capacity for enlightenment. While Kant thought maturity was a positive achievement, enabling people to think for themselves independently of authorities, Goethe here implies that it means discarding the ancient ties of love and loyalty and pursuing one's own interests with no regard for anyone else.

Goethe's dramas often convey a deep historical pessimism which runs throughout his life and is underlined by his literary portrayal of kings and aristocrats. As early as *Werther* (1774), the hierarchical order, while said to be inevitable, is shown to be stifling. Werther is turned out of a noble gathering because convention dictates that after a certain hour no commoners may be present, and finds his humiliation is the talk of the town. In *Wilhelm Meister* the actors receive patronage from a Count who fails to provide them with proper accommodation and displays them to his guests only after his horses and dogs. From the 1790s we find a series of ineffectual monarchs. In the humorous beast-epic *Reineke Fuchs* (*Reynard the Fox*, 1794), the traditional king of beasts, the lion, is helpless before the cunning of Reynard, who typifies the cynical calculation that Goethe thought characteristic of the modern age. The King in *The Natural Daughter* is equally helpless. And in *Faust II*, when Faust visits the Emperor's court, the elaborate ceremonial disguises a financial crisis, which the devilish Mephistopheles (generally called Mephisto for short) solves by inventing paper money, a currency supported by the treasure supposed to be buried throughout the Empire. We learn later that this fraudulent expedient has merely postponed the Empire's bankruptcy.

Under the guise of fiction, Goethe imagines several visionary schemes of social reform. In the later chapters of *Wilhelm Meister*, Wilhelm visits the estate of the aristocrat Lothario, where the mysterious Society of the Tower is based. Lothario, an enlightened nobleman who has fought on the American side in the War of Independence, wants to abolish the feudal structure of society. Instead of receiving his estate as a fief from his prince, and receiving dues from his tenants, he would like a system in which his tenants paid taxes to him, he in turn paid taxes to the State, and had the freedom to divide his estate among his family as he pleased, thus stimulating economic activity. A self-styled patriot, he is concerned about the good of society as a whole. There is an extreme contrast with Wilhelm's friend Werner, the representative of the commercial middle class, who buys part of Lothario's estate. Werner confesses that he has never thought about the state. Earlier, Werner has expressed the following credo: 'conduct your business, acquire money, enjoy yourself with your family, and don't bother about anybody else unless you can use them to your advantage' (V, 2). Werner, who ranks double-entry book-keeping among the highest human achievements, clearly belongs to the modern age of selfish calculation that Goethe repeatedly condemns. Hope for the future cannot lie in the commercial classes, only in an enlightened aristocracy. Lothario is moreover prepared to marry outside his own class and welcome the socially mobile Wilhelm into it as his brother-in-law. This social utopia may be seen as Goethe's positive, but admittedly impracticable, answer to the French Revolution.

A yet more ambitious plan is put forward at the end of *Faust*. From the wreckage of the Empire, Faust—now a hundred years old, and blind—obtains a tract of coastal land which he enlarges by reclaiming more land from the sea. Faust now appears as a distinctively modern figure. He is a capitalist entrepreneur, who employs large numbers of men on his engineering project, and enriches himself with the proceeds of theft and piracy conducted by Mephisto. But before we condemn him, we need to see that Goethe is here addressing a problem that in a complex modern society becomes acute: the problem of *agency*. In a leadership role, you direct dozens, perhaps thousands, of other people to put your wishes into practice. As your employees and/or subordinates, they are dependent on you. But you are also dependent on them. You cannot constantly supervise them all, so they must use their own initiative, but in doing so they may spoil or even wreck your plans.

This happens with Faust. His chief overseer is Mephisto (though the land reclamation seems to depend on labour power, not on magic). Faust tells Mephisto to remove an old couple, Philemon and Baucis, whose cottage is situated at a viewpoint he wants for himself, to another location which he has designated for them. Mephisto, however, shortens the task by burning down the cottage with the couple inside. This is a grave crime; but it is one for which Faust is ultimately, not immediately, responsible. His blindness may be taken to symbolize his limited awareness of what is going on under his rule.

Faust plans yet more ambitious works. He wants to drain a swamp and thus create further space for a new society whose inhabitants will live in freedom, kept alert by constantly having to defend their territory against the sea.

> I long to see that multitude, and stand
> With a free people on free land! (lines 11579–80)

This vision of a future free society has divided critical opinion. Some have thought it banal: 'After Greece,' said the American philosopher George Santayana, 'Faust has a vision of Holland.' Yet in Goethe's day the Netherlands were the pre-eminent example of a free republic which had successfully fought for its liberty. Others find the vision unattractive, or think it is undercut by irony, or maintain that a society made possible by the ruthless capitalism evoked earlier, and by engineering works which have cost many lives, cannot really be free. But perhaps Goethe is suggesting a more difficult message. Capitalism is not benign. It originates as robbery. But it brings nature under humanity's control and it creates the wealth which is necessary to support a complex society. The redistribution of that wealth is necessary to create a free society and, as Marx put it in *Capital*, 'that development of human power which is an end in itself, the true realm of freedom, which, however, can blossom forth only with this realm of necessity as its basis'. Injustice and inequality are the unavoidable basis for eventual justice and equality. There was never any way of reaching a free society without going through the horrors of capitalism first.

Goethe has not written an apologia for capitalism, but presented a vision of life after capitalism. It may have been inspired by Goethe's knowledge of the utopian society imagined by Henri de Saint-Simon (1760–1825) in which the latest technical resources were to be harnessed in order to eliminate poverty. It reflects also Goethe's enthusiasm for great engineering projects. In 1827 he wished he could live to see canals driven through the isthmuses of Panama and Suez, and another connecting the Rhine with the Danube (to Eckermann, 21 February 1827). The play strikes a darker note, however, for Goethe has acknowledged the tragic losses demanded by modernization. Good things are swept away. The simple life of the kindly old couple, next door to a chapel, is wantonly destroyed. This part of *Faust* has been called 'the tragedy of the developer' and read as prophetic. In modern projects for urban renewal, from Baron Haussmann's rebuilding of Paris to Robert Moses' flattening of whole districts of New York to make way for the Cross-Bronx Expressway, the grandiose vision of the developer has been realized only at the cost of destroying old neighbourhoods and their history. If in his recorded comments Goethe often seems a diehard opponent of the modern world, the great moments of his literature show that his imagination responded not only to the old but also to the new.

Napoleon and the daemonic

We may understand the late Faust better if we consider Goethe's attitude to Napoleon. With his usual independence of mind, he persisted in admiring Napoleon, the invader of Germany and conqueror of Prussia, whom patriots denounced as a devil risen from hell. For him, Napoleon was the hero who had defeated the French Revolution and replaced anarchy with a social order which Goethe hoped would prove permanent. More than that, Napoleon was a superhuman figure, 'the highest phenomenon that was possible in history'. 'His life was the striding of a demi-god from battle to battle and from victory to victory', Goethe later said to Eckermann (11 March 1828). Goethe's meeting with Napoleon at

Erfurt on 2 October 1808, and again in Weimar on 6 October, was one of the supreme moments of his life. Napoleon awarded him the Légion d'Honneur, which he proudly wore at every opportunity. Hence he deeply disliked the often furious German nationalism that grew up during Napoleon's occupation, triumphed over his downfall, and would flourish for the next century and a half.

To Goethe, Napoleon was the ultimate embodiment of the force that he called 'the daemonic'. This had nothing to do with devils; Goethe found in classical authors, especially Plato, the 'daemon' as a mysterious, morally ambivalent force that could determine a person's life. The term served Goethe to denote a power that reason could not explain, that was neither good nor evil, and that was embodied in certain charismatic individuals. Other daemonic characters included Duke Carl August, Lord Byron, Mozart, and such fictitious persons as Egmont and Faust. The daemonic, according to Goethe's autobiography, is 'a power, not contrary to the moral order of the world, but running athwart it', and the people who incarnate it radiate an 'enormous force' and 'exert unbelievable power over all creatures, even over the elements'.

An exceptional figure such as Napoleon therefore could not be judged by moral standards. 'Extraordinary people like Napoleon are outside morality,' Goethe said in 1807; 'they operate like physical causes such as fire and water.' The same applies to Faust as he storms through the world. Hence the verses from the *West-Eastern Divan*, where, as we have seen, the Central Asian conqueror Timur stands in for Napoleon, and Goethe is clearly recalling his own conversations with the Emperor:

Übermacht, Ihr könnt es spüren,
Ist nicht aus der Welt zu bannen;
Mir gefällt zu conversiren
Mit Gescheiten, mit Tyrannen.

> Overwhelming power, as you can feel, cannot be banished from the world. I enjoy conversing with intelligent people, with tyrants.

In his idealization of Napoleon, Goethe may again be seen as prophetic, this time in a disturbing way. Especially in the first half of the 20th century, many writers dreamed of strong leaders who would sweep away the petty dreariness of mass democracy and restore a heroic past, 'before the merchant and the clerk | Breathed on the world with timid breath' (W. B. Yeats, 'At Galway Races'). Goethe's cult of Napoleon shows what power such fantasies can hold.

Chapter 5
Tragedy

Modern tragedy

Goethe lived in a great age of tragedy-writing. While the tragedies produced in 18th-century Britain and France—Samuel Johnson's *Irene*, John Home's *Douglas*, the many tragedies of Voltaire—are now read only by scholars, German playwrights created a large body of tragic drama that still holds the stage. The tradition of German tragedy runs from Lessing, who introduced domestic tragedy with *Miss Sara Sampson* (1755), via Goethe, Schiller, Heinrich von Kleist, Franz Grillparzer, Georg Büchner, down to the political and historical dramas of Friedrich Hebbel; and it was, though not a German, still a Germanic dramatist, the Norwegian Henrik Ibsen, who created an internationally influential form of realist tragedy. Goethe's place in this tradition is assured especially by his most famous work, *Faust*, which is explicitly called a tragedy; its two parts are subtitled respectively the First and Second Parts of the Tragedy.

Some critics, however, question whether modern plays can properly be called tragedies. They maintain that tragedy presupposes belief in a supernatural reality, whether fate or the gods, which is inscrutable and mysterious, but which renders the tragic catastrophe inevitable. After Shakespeare and Racine, they argue, so-called tragedies lack this cosmic background, and so their catastrophes do not overawe us with a feeling of necessity. The events could have turned out differently. Ibsen's Nora in *A Doll's House* could have been reconciled with her husband; she was not compelled to walk out of her marriage. It is also sometimes claimed that tragic drama requires dignity, and that its personnel should therefore be people of high social rank. Ibsen's housewives, doctors, and bank managers cannot possibly impress us as much as King Lear or Oedipus.

Although these arguments are, in my view, mistaken, they do start from a historical fact—that modern tragedy is a product of the Enlightenment. The thinkers of the Enlightenment subjected religious claims to the tests of rational argument and historical scholarship. A little logic showed that the Christian conception of God was self-contradictory: if he was both supremely powerful and completely good, why had he let the world get into its present dreadful state? And if the world's deficiencies were blamed on humanity's wickedness, how could that explain natural disasters such as the Lisbon earthquake? Meanwhile the 'Higher Criticism' asked how the Bible came to be written, and found that far from an infallible sacred book, it was a very unreliable account of historical events, mingled with mythology. Between the demonstrable truths of history and the claims of faith, said Lessing, there was a 'broad and ugly ditch' which he for one could not leap over. Many intelligent people in the 18th century, including Goethe, could no longer take the assertions of Christianity seriously. Tragedy would still be written, but it had to be a post-Christian form of tragedy, no longer set against a cosmic background. Words such as 'heaven', 'hell', 'angel', 'devil', were still used, but only for rhetorical effect, without supernatural content. Goethe seems to restore the cosmic background in *Faust*, which begins with a 'Prologue in Heaven', shows Faust in the company of the devil Mephistopheles, and ends with his ascent to heaven; but these cosmic elements are a deliberate fiction, at times ironic, at other times symbolic.

Enlightenment thinkers were interested in emotion as well as reason. They saw humanity as primarily social. The bonds of society were sympathy and fellow-feeling. The tragic hero should not be distanced from the audience by royal status, but should be a fellow human being. 'If we feel sympathy for kings,' wrote Lessing in his *Hamburg Dramaturgy* (1766–7), 'it is because they are human beings, not because they are kings.' Since the Enlightenment, therefore, tragedy has been democratic. An ordinary person of lowly status, like Faust's lover Gretchen, is fully capable of tragic dignity.

Goethe's tragic themes

To understand Goethe's approach to tragedy, we need to deal with an apparent contradiction. In a famous letter, Goethe told Schiller that he could not write a tragedy. 'I do not know myself well enough to tell whether I could write a real tragedy, but the very undertaking alarms me and I am almost convinced that the mere attempt could destroy me' (9 December 1797). Yet by this time he had written many tragedies. In his first published play, *Götz von Berlichingen*, the hero dies, aware that the values by which he has lived are now obsolete. *Clavigo* (1774) ends with the deaths of the hero and his lover. *Werther* can be described as a tragic novel, especially in the first version where the protagonist's self-centredness is less obvious. In *Egmont* (begun in 1775, completed and published in 1788) the hero is betrayed, imprisoned, and executed, though with the prospect of becoming a national symbol and inspiring his fellow Netherlanders to fight for their freedom. The earliest surviving version of *Faust*, known as the *Urfaust*, centres on what is called the 'Gretchen Tragedy': Faust abandons his lover; she is imprisoned for killing their child; when Faust tries to save her with the Devil's help on the eve of her execution, she rebuffs him and throws herself on God's mercy. And the classical drama *Torquato Tasso* (1790) is the tragedy of a poet who, unable to cope with the intrigues and deceptions practised at his patron's court, ends on the verge of madness. So Goethe's statement to Schiller cannot be taken at face value. Its meaning will emerge once we have glanced at the tragic themes and plots that Goethe favours.

Frequently we find a central character with exceptional gifts, and a charismatic appeal to the people around him, trapped in a world that is too small for him, and brought low by the intrigues of lesser people. These exceptional figures are not superhuman; they are people of the same stuff as ourselves, in networks of recognizable human relationships. Götz von Berlichingen is a late-medieval knight admired for his courage, his generosity, and his attacks on rich people who oppress the poor; he is also a loving husband and the father of a rather disappointing son. Egmont is admired by the Netherlanders as a military leader, and loved by his middle-class girl-friend Klärchen. Götz is brought down partly by the obsessive intrigues of his disloyal friend, the careerist and courtier Weislingen, and Egmont falls victim to the deceitful Spanish occupiers whom he was guileless enough to trust. The image of prison keeps recurring. Götz is besieged in his castle, captured and confined, set free by his allies, but finally placed under house arrest, where he dies. Egmont is last seen in prison, shortly before his execution. Werther calls the world a prison, but consoles himself by thinking that he can escape from it at any time by suicide (22 May 1771). The scholar Faust calls his study a 'prison' and finds all of earthly life confining (lines 398, 1544–5).

Characters in these plays are often inwardly divided. Weislingen both admires and envies Götz. His inner duality is brought out by his attraction to two contrasting women: briefly engaged to Götz's sister Marie, he abandons her for the sophisticated noblewoman Adelheid. Clavigo is another indecisive character: he breaks off his engagement, then resumes it, then breaks it again on being persuaded by a ruthlessly amoral friend that a humble marriage will destroy his career prospects. Of these divided selves, the most famous is Faust:

> In me there are two souls, alas, and their
> Division tears my life in two.
> One loves the world, it clutches her, it binds
> Itself to her, clinging with furious lust;
> The other longs to soar beyond the dust
> Into the realm of high ancestral minds. (lines 1102–7)

The divided self often incurs guilt. The unfaithfulness shown by Weislingen and Clavigo is commonly supposed to express Goethe's guilt towards Friederike Brion, as is the betrayal of Gretchen by Faust. The latter, however, is portrayed much more intensely. Thanks to his devilish companion Mephistopheles, Faust has magically become thirty years younger. Bursting with libido, he promptly becomes enamoured of Gretchen, a girl from a modest background, who inflames his passion further by pertly rebuffing his advances. Their love soon becomes robustly physical, but it leads Faust into ever deeper guilt: a sleeping-draught administered to Gretchen's mother poisons her; Faust kills Gretchen's brother in a duel; finally, obliged to flee, distracted by Mephisto (and also becoming rather bored with Gretchen), he forgets about her long enough for her to bear his child, drown it, and be arrested for the capital crime of infanticide. The final scene of *Faust I*, 'Prison', is the most searing scene Goethe ever wrote. Gretchen, driven mad by her sufferings, at first fails to recognize Faust when he comes to save her. Ignoring his pleas to accompany him, she insists on reliving, and making him experience vicariously, the traumatic sequence of events that culminated in her drowning her child. Unable to escape the spectacle of her suffering, Faust is reduced to wishing he had never been born.

This scene helps to make sense of Goethe's puzzling statement that the attempt to write a tragedy might destroy him. It shows us, with scarcely bearable vividness, the naked pain that Gretchen suffers, condemned to keep reliving her nightmarish experiences, and also the agony of guilt that Faust suffers in knowing that his actions condemned her to it. It is on a par with the scene in *King Lear* where the mad Lear carries the body of his daughter Cordelia onto the stage and at first refuses to believe that she is dead. One might well be shocked at oneself on finding one had written such an agonizing scene. When Goethe published *Faust I* in 1808 (some scenes appeared as *Faust: A Fragment* in 1790), he toned it down: he changed the original prose into verse, in order to distance the reader from the emotions, and after Mephisto's gloating last word on Gretchen, 'She is condemned', he introduced a Voice from Above which says 'Is saved!' So although Gretchen will be executed, we are reassured that she will not go to hell.

A curious feature of Goethe's tragic writing is that when he presents perpetrators and victims, he sometimes focuses on the victim's suffering, as with Gretchen, but more often on that of the perpetrator. Weislingen and Clavigo receive more attention than the women they betray. A signal example occurs in *Wilhelm Meister's Apprenticeship*. There, Wilhelm abandons his lover Mariane in the mistaken belief that she was two-timing him. Mariane vanishes, and we learn only much later that she died in misery. Wilhelm is so upset by her supposed unfaithfulness that he suffers a nervous breakdown from which it takes him months to recover. She is not the only person to whom, unwittingly, he does irreparable harm. But the novel treats his experiences, not morally, but medically. He is not blameworthy, but ill, and he must be helped to recover. In *Faust*, too, Goethe soon transfers attention from Gretchen to her lover, showing what a terrible experience it was for Faust to find out that he betrayed her.

Torquato Tasso

Before looking at the many problems that *Faust* poses, we need to give special consideration to one of Goethe's supreme masterpieces, the tragedy *Torquato Tasso*. Goethe worked on it intermittently during the 1780s and published it in 1790. It is among the first German plays based on the life of a real poet, the Italian Torquato Tasso (1544–95), whose works include the great epic poem about the First Crusade, *Gerusalemme liberata* (*Jerusalem Delivered*, published 1581). Goethe thus unwittingly founded the genre of literary fictions about real artists ('Künstlerdramen', 'Künstlerromane') which remains popular in Germany down to the present day. His choice means that he does not have to convince us that his hero is a genius (as Thomas Mann did with his fictional composer Leverkühn in *Doktor Faustus*). And since tragedies traditionally deal with historical or mythical subjects, whereas comedies present subjects invented by the dramatist, *Tasso*'s foundation in historical reality already invites us to approach it as a tragedy.

The historical Tasso was supported by the Duke of Ferrara but was difficult, suspicious, unruly, occasionally violent. At the very time he was completing the *Gerusalemme liberata*, he was confined from 1579 to 1586 in a hospital, partly as cure and partly as punishment, and certainly suffered spells of insanity, perhaps made worse by long periods of solitary confinement. Though Goethe's version is largely faithful to the facts, his Tasso also recalls a more recent figure, Jean-Jacques Rousseau (1712–78). Rousseau's tendency to paranoia was made clear in his *Confessions* (1782), but he was famous especially as a pungent critic of modern civilization. His prize-winning *Discourse on the Moral Effects of the Arts and Sciences* (1750) argued that so-called progress merely corrupted the primitive innocence of humanity by creating artificial needs and sophisticated vices. Goethe's Tasso recalls such views by his eulogy of the 'golden age' when 'what pleases is permitted' (line 994), and his unease among the constraints of civilization when, as his friend the Princess reminds him, 'what is proper is permitted' (line 1006).

The morbid suspicion shown by Goethe's Tasso has some justification. Coming from the impoverished minor nobility, he has a marginal place at the ducal court of Ferrara. His employer treats him indulgently, but wants him, self-contradictorily, both to be more sociable and to get on with his poem. He is attractive to both the Princess and her friend Leonore Sanvitale, but in different ways. Leonore, whose manipulative charm Tasso sees through, wants to entice him to her husband's court at Florence and to exploit his feelings so that he will address love-poems to her that will make her name immortal. Her rival the Princess is more enigmatic. An intelligent, well-educated woman with a long history of illness and a tendency to depression, she loves Tasso but never intends him to be more than a soul-mate. Not thinking that he might want his love for her to be physically consummated, she keeps him as a frustrated admirer, as Charlotte von Stein did Goethe. Her indiscreet language, however, leads Tasso into forgetting the social gulf between them and embracing her—a social blunder which must end their relationship for ever.

Court life also generates rivalry. Tasso's polar opposite is an older man, the diplomat Antonio, who has long been irritated by Tasso's childish behaviour and is seriously annoyed when he returns from successfully conducting difficult territorial negotiations in Rome only to find Tasso being crowned with laurels by female admirers. Unable to be the centre of attention, Antonio hurtfully belittles Tasso's achievement. Persuaded by the Princess to forgive Antonio, Tasso next day effusively offers him friendship. Antonio, too repelled by Tasso's puppy-like enthusiasm to recognize the generosity behind it, responds with increasingly wounding reproofs, until Tasso, goaded beyond endurance, draws his sword and challenges Antonio to a duel. The Duke separates them, sends Tasso to his room, rebukes Antonio gently but effectively, and makes him promise to mend fences with Tasso. But by now it is too late. Tasso slides into paranoia, misinterprets almost everything said to him, and finally disgraces himself irreparably by assaulting the Princess. Antonio, now showing his decent side, tries to encourage Tasso, but is finally speechless in the face of Tasso's misery, which is no less distressing for being partially self-inflicted. Lost for words, he takes Tasso's hand in a silent gesture of basic human solidarity.

What makes this a tragedy? Partly, the situation of the poet, whose contemplative character makes him out of place in society. His poetic gift is resented by the ungifted, and even those who appreciate it want to exploit him; as his presence adds lustre to the Ferrarese court, the Duke does not want to lose him to Florence or Rome. Coming from a relatively modest background, Tasso cannot cope with the subtle intrigues always going on at court, nor with the patronizing superiority assumed by Antonio; he resorts either to open anger, or to attempts at courtly dissimulation which are ill-judged and only make his situation worse. He is irresolute, like Goethe's earlier heroes: he has no sooner handed over his great poem than he wants it back in order to tinker with it; resolving to leave Ferrara, he vacillates among Florence, Rome, or Naples. Like earlier heroes, too, he feels imprisoned: 'Is the free spirit imprisoned in the palace?' (line 1348). Again like them, he inflicts irreparable harm on someone he loves. If the Princess kept him dangling, her motives may include emotional fragility, and fear not just of sex but of involvement with life, which can only be heightened by Tasso's assault. None of these factors, however, has the *necessity* sometimes thought requisite for tragedy. Not all poets are as helpless as Tasso, not all courtiers as exploitative as the Ferrarese. The catastrophe did not have to happen. It results from the mismatch among *this* particular group of complex individuals. Does that make it any less tragic?

Tasso differs from a familiar model of tragedy, however, in lacking catharsis. Aristotle in his *Poetics* famously described tragedy as 'effecting through pity and fear the catharsis of such emotions'. 'Catharsis' appears to be a medical term implying purgation. Our emotions are first aroused, then relieved by the tragic catastrophe, leaving us in what Milton called 'calm of mind, all passion spent' (*Samson Agonistes*, 1671). *Tasso*, however, may leave the audience feeling as distressed as Antonio. Not only is the situation unresolved, but, if we know Tasso's biography, we know that he is facing seven years in a madhouse.

In rejecting catharsis, Goethe has recognized that tragedy as described by Aristotle is a highly artificial literary construction. Real suffering seldom mounts to a climax to be followed by peace. Either it drags on dismally, or the sufferer succeeds in recovering and moving forward. Goethe has brought art dangerously close to reality. He has denied us the false consolation that comes from a dramatic structure leading up to catharsis, and made us confront the reality of incurable emotional suffering. He has softened it only by writing *Tasso* not in the prose of real life but in blank verse of extraordinary delicacy, precision, and beauty—rather as he softened the 'Prison' scene in the *Urfaust* by recasting it in verse.

To see what Goethe offers instead of catharsis, let us glance back to *Wilhelm Meister's Apprenticeship*. Long after abandoning Mariane, Wilhelm learns that she was faithful and that she has died, leaving him their child. Wilhelm has ruined Mariane's life, as Faust has Gretchen's, and neither can ever make things better. In Greek tragedy, this might have led to a spectacular act of atonement, as when Sophocles' Oedipus, on learning that he is unwittingly guilty of parricide and incest, tears out his own eyes. But what good would it do Wilhelm, or anyone else, if he were to mutilate himself as a symbolic penance? Instead, he does what good he can in the situation, by assuming responsibility for his son (and evidently proving an excellent father). The implied message may seem mundane: instead of futile lamentations, move on, and do all the good you can. In real life, this would be the right course, and though some aspects of *Meister* are highly artificial, here Goethe is once again bringing fiction disconcertingly close to reality.

Faust: moving beyond tragedy

His *Faust* project accompanied Goethe throughout his life. The historical Faust, registered as a student at Heidelberg in 1507, was a wandering scholar who acquired a reputation for magic. Legend said that he sold his soul to the Devil in exchange for twenty-four years of power and pleasure, during which he visited the Emperor's court and possessed the most beautiful woman who ever lived, Helen of Troy, but was finally damned. This story, disapprovingly recounted in a popular book of 1587, found its way to Britain and inspired Christopher Marlowe's *Doctor Faustus*. By Goethe's time it had become the material of a popular puppet-play. In his 'Sturm und Drang' phase of the early 1770s, Goethe planned to adapt this material and combine it with a realistic tragedy about Faust's seduction of a young woman who was then executed for infanticide. From Goethe's earliest surviving version, known as the *Urfaust*, it is still unclear how the two narratives would be spliced together. In the completed drama, however, of which *Faust I* was published in 1808 and *Faust II* after Goethe's death in 1832, not only are they integrated in unexpected ways, but their tragic potential is richly developed.

The *Urfaust*, and hence the main action of the completed drama, opens with the scholar Faust in his prison-like study, lamenting in rough-hewn colloquial verse (*Knittelvers*) that he has studied everything and learnt nothing. His dissatisfaction with the limits of knowledge soon grows into a frustration with the limitations of earthly life. Wanting to commune with spirits, and even to become a spirit himself, he uses magic to evoke a vision of the entire cosmos; but its serenity leaves him wanting to share the dynamic energies of nature, and so he summons up their embodiment, the Earth Spirit, claiming to be its equal. The Spirit, however, scornfully rejects his pretensions and vanishes, leaving Faust in a state of near-suicidal despair and ripe to be tempted by Mephisto.

In *Faust I* Goethe has made two major innovations to the Faust story. First: before meeting Faust, we have had a 'Prologue in Heaven', where the Lord addresses the angels. Here Goethe is following the Book of Job, which tells us: 'Again there was a day when the sons of God came to present themselves before the Lord, and Satan came also among them to present himself before the Lord' (Job 2:1). While the Biblical Job was a test case for human piety in misfortune, his counterpart Faust is the guinea-pig in a different experiment. The Lord, a relaxed and humorous adherent of the Enlightenment, thinks that Faust's seemingly futile strivings are a necessary stage on his path towards clarity. The nihilist Mephisto, however, thinks that all human effort is mere folly, and that the heavenly light of reason with which the Lord endowed humankind has merely given them new ways of being bestial. He offers the Lord a wager that he will convert Faust to his own nihilism; the Lord takes him on, confident of winning.

By this prologue, Goethe has altered the fundamental terms of the Faust story. It is no longer a drama of good versus evil. Good and evil are no longer antitheses. 'What we call evil,' Goethe said in his 1771 Shakespeare lecture, 'is only the other side of the good, and is necessary to its existence.' Hence Mephisto is allowed into Heaven. He is the Lord's secret agent. He prods and pushes people into action when they might otherwise choose a comfortable life instead of developing their abilities.

So Mephisto, it seems, is actually sent to Faust by the Lord, and the pact they sign merges into a wager, corresponding to the wager placed in Heaven. Faust, devastated by the Earth Spirit's rejection, maintains that nothing on earth has any lasting value. He challenges Mephisto to prove him wrong:

> If ever to the moment I shall say:
> Beautiful moment, do not pass away!
> Then you may forge your chains to bind me,
> Then I will put my life behind me...(lines 1700–3)

Although Mephisto agrees, he is happy to accept Faust's challenge, reckoning that he must win whatever happens. If Faust finds something valuable in life, its value will turn out to be illusory, and Faust will fall into nihilism. Or if he finds nothing valuable, he will fall into nihilism anyway. So *Faust* asks whether there is anything truly valuable in the world. And the world, despite the tongue-in-cheek cosmic apparatus, is the post-Christian world we live in, where nothing is any longer underwritten by a supernatural guarantee.

Goethe's second great innovation follows from this. For if Faust is to seek value in the world, he must emerge from his study and explore the world as it is. The traditional fantastic adventures—visiting the Emperor's court, marrying Helen of Troy—are deferred till Part II. At present, Faust wants to get to know ordinary human life:

> I've purged the lust for knowledge from my soul;
> From now on it shall shun no sort of pain,
> And in my inner self I will sustain
> The experience allotted to the whole
> Race of mankind...(lines 1768–72)

We might wonder why he needs the Devil's help for this, but as an elderly scholar with a long beard, he needs to be rejuvenated. A quick visit to a witch's kitchen does the trick, and Faust and Mephisto are off on their adventures. Wanting Faust to be disappointed, Mephisto offers only such banal pleasures as a drinking party in a Leipzig pub, and at first he thinks Gretchen will prove equally trivial; but lust becomes love, and the Gretchen tragedy runs its course.

Before its end, however, Faust is compelled to recognize what he has done. Mephisto tries to distract him from Gretchen by carrying him off to the celebration of Walpurgisnacht—the night before 1 May, when all the German witches assemble on the flat top of the Brocken, the mountain in the Harz that Goethe climbed in 1777. But even there his unconscious gives him a vision of Gretchen in chains. Early the following morning, in the powerful prose scene 'A Gloomy Day. Open Country', Faust denounces Mephisto for letting Gretchen suffer; but Mephisto, with truly devilish callousness, but also with justice, rebukes him for trying to transcend human limits and keep company with spirits—'Why try to fly if you've no head for heights?'—and concludes unanswerably: 'Who was it who ruined her? I, or you?' This recognition of his wrong-doing and its consequences is called in tragic theory *anagnorisis*, and is followed in many dramas by an act of atonement like the self-blinding of Oedipus.

Not in *Faust*, however. After the intense agony of the 'Prison' scene, an unspecified time passes, and at the beginning of Part II we find Faust lying on an Alpine meadow, attended by charming spirits who pity his distress and sing him to sleep. When he wakes the next morning, Faust is refreshed and ready to continue his career, thanks to the healing power of nature. Now this may seem unfair, indeed morally offensive. After all, Faust is responsible for Gretchen's misery and death. One might feel that he should be punished, or at least have the decency to be emotionally devastated. However, it seems he has been punished enough by the agony of confronting Gretchen in prison. Thereafter his moral failure is treated as a medical problem. Not atonement, but healing, is prescribed. A spectacular act of atonement would do no good: it wouldn't bring Gretchen back to life, and it would only prevent Faust from achieving his potential and, perhaps, doing some good in the world. Goethe is here moving beyond catharsis and beyond tragedy.

Healed by nature's soothing influence, Faust is not just his old self. In a symbolic sequence he tries first to look straight at the rising sun, cannot bear the sight, and turns round to contemplate a waterfall in which the sun's rays are reflected. He concludes:

> I watch a mirror here of man's whole story,
> And plain it speaks, ponder it as you will:
> Our life's a spectrum-sheen of borrowed glory. (lines 4725–7)

In other words, Faust has realized that he cannot reach superhuman status. Neither the company of spirits, nor the direct view of the sun, are for him.

There is no space here to explore the marvels and mysteries of Part II. Accompanied and helped by Mephisto, Faust visits the Imperial court and sorts out the Empire's financial problems; he experiences a classical counterpart to the German Walpurgisnacht, where all the monsters from Greek mythology appear; he marries Helen of Troy and has a son, Euphorion, who inherits his father's former aspiring spirit but crashes to earth like Icarus; and finally he appears as the visionary founder of a new society.

However, when Faust conceives his final project of social reform, he is already blind, and though he gives orders for workmen to begin digging, the clinking of spades he hears in fact indicates that they are digging his grave. This does not negate the value of his plans, but it reminds us that he is both literally and symbolically blind, and also that he is tragically unable to overcome human limitations. Whatever his exalted plans for humanity, and despite his long and uniquely adventurous life, Faust himself is mortal, and mortality finally catches up with him.

What happens to his wager with Mephisto (and to Mephisto's wager with the Lord)? Has Faust found any value in life? He certainly has—first in Gretchen's love, later in Helen's—but the Devil, being literal-minded, waits till Faust uses the exact words specified in the wager. Imagining the society of the future, Faust says:

> Then to the moment I might say:
> Beautiful moment, do not pass away! (lines 11581–2)

Mephisto, not realizing that the words are spoken in invisible quotation marks, thinks his moment has come. But when angels descend from heaven, the sight of their pretty bottoms distracts the paedophilic Mephisto and gives him an inkling that there may really be such a thing as love after all. When Mephisto is not looking, Faust's immortal part is carried up to heaven, leaving Mephisto with the useless mortal part and the bitter realization that he has utterly failed.

The heaven Faust enters is wholly different from the setting of the Prologue. None of the persons of the Trinity is present. Adoration is directed at a being who suggests the Virgin Mary but, unlike her, is called a goddess. Even the boundaries of heaven are unclear: we move imperceptibly from a mountain-top populated by holy hermits to celestial spheres inhabited by angels and redeemed souls, including that of Gretchen. The Christian imagery, suggested by Dante's *Paradiso* and by frescoes Goethe saw at Pisa, has the same status as the Greek mythology that was liberally used earlier in the poem. Goethe explained to Eckermann that in evoking matters that lie beyond our knowledge, he could easily have fallen into mere vagueness if he had not borrowed Christian figures with their firm outlines (6 June 1831; see Figure 7).

The poem's cosmology is Neoplatonic. The ultimate reality can only be conveyed in negative language: one can only say what it

7. Angels on a fresco from the Campo Santo in Pisa, indicating how Goethe imagined the final scene of *Faust II*.

is not. The force that draws us towards it is desire. Hence the famously enigmatic closing lines: 'Eternal Womanhood | Draws us on high', which, from a present-day perspective, unfortunately limit the scope of Goethe's cosmic Eros by implying that its appeal is to men. Faust owes his redemption to the fact that, despite Mephisto's efforts, he has never abandoned desire but has always striven for something that lay beyond him. He owes it, perhaps even more, to Gretchen's intercession on his behalf. Existence after death is here imagined, not as a Christian last judgement after which the saved praise God monotonously for all eternity, but as a continual process of transformation and purification. Tragedy has no place here; we have moved beyond it.

Chapter 6
Religion

In *Faust I*, the naively pious Gretchen asks her lover a difficult question which has become proverbial in German as the 'Gretchenfrage': 'Do you believe in God?' Faust's reply is eloquent. God is all around us: how can one say one *believes* in him, as though this were a purely intellectual matter? And since God is all around us, how can one *not* believe in him? Gretchen misses the point: 'That's more or less what the priest says, only in different words.' But Faust's profession of faith, which can fairly be attributed also to Goethe, is not what most priests would say. It is a product of the Enlightenment.

Goethe and the Enlightenment

The great intellectual movement that we now call the Enlightenment developed in the late 17th century. Horrified by the religious wars which had devastated Germany and shaken France and Britain, the Enlightenment relied on the methods of empirical science, rational inquiry, and historical interpretation. Galileo, Newton, and other leaders of the 17th-century scientific revolution had revealed many of the secrets of nature with mathematical certainty, but their methods could not be applied to religious claims. Many enlightened thinkers concluded that religion was a matter for the individual, and that differences in religion should be treated tolerantly; a radical fringe, especially in France, attacked religious belief as baseless and absurd, and sought also to demolish what they considered the tyrannical and fraudulent authority of the Churches. Meanwhile, the historical study of the Bible treated it not as the infallible word of God, but as a collection of books written by human authors at specific times and places, and often distorted by mistakes in copying and translation. The mainstream Enlightenment, outside and sometimes within the Churches, sought to retain the moral and emotional core of religion but purify it of implausible supernatural claims and superstitious accretions.

Frankfurt, where Goethe was brought up, was a Protestant city, where the Lutheran Church held sway. Orthodox Lutheranism was rigid and dogmatic. It angrily refused to admit that modern science and historical scholarship had undermined the Bible's claim to absolute truth. The young Goethe was exposed to the orthodox doctrines, as we can see from the poem he wrote at 16, 'Poetic Thoughts on Jesus Christ's Descent into Hell, written on request by J.W.G.', of which he was later ashamed. But even as a boy he rebelled against what he afterwards called 'a kind of dry morality'. He gained a deep familiarity with the Bible, enjoying 'the rugged naturalness of the Old Testament and the tender simplicity of the New', while noticing the contradictions and absurdities present in both.

His father's extensive library, however, also enabled Goethe to discover key Enlightenment texts, especially the *Philosophical Dictionary* by Pierre Bayle (1647–1706). This huge book, one of most-read works of the early 18th century, is ostensibly a biographical guide to philosophers and theologians from ancient times to the present, but tucked away in its copious footnotes are many witty and devastating comments on Christian orthodoxy. As a student in Leipzig, Goethe also read Voltaire, but Voltaire's blatant mockery of religion was less to his taste.

Like many young people, Goethe went through what is called a 'religious phase'. In 1768, studying at Leipzig, he fell ill, suffered a lung haemorrhage, and returned home to spend eighteen months convalescing. Illness combined with depression helped draw him under the influence of his mother's Pietist friend Susanna von Klettenberg. Pietism was a movement within Lutheranism which (like Methodism in England) sought a more inward, emotional form of religion based on an intimate relationship to God. It helped Klettenberg, a warm, cheerful, natural person, to accept illness patiently and to find satisfaction in a wide range of occult and mystical writings, whose influence on Goethe is still under dispute. His Pietist phase was good for Goethe. It taught him what the religious life felt like from the inside, and immunized him against the shallow contempt for religion that he disliked in Voltaire. In *Wilhelm Meister's Apprenticeship* he included an autobiographical narrative by a devout lady, 'Confessions of a Beautiful Soul', based on his recollections of Klettenberg, though told with some irony of which the beautiful soul is happily unaware.

Goethe could not stay long among the Pietists. His positive view of humanity was too optimistic for their liking. He could not undergo the conviction of sin which they considered essential for a truly Christian life. In a letter of 17 January 1769, Goethe describes a Pietist meeting, with wine and sausages provided, where hymns were sung to the piano and the flute: 'Mellin [a devotee] and I were standing at the back and could not see properly; "Why is it so dark here!" I said, lighting a chandelier that hung over us, and then it was nice and bright.' This introduction of light into a religious scene seems to symbolize Goethe's desire to reconcile religion with the Enlightenment.

However, his Pietist phase strengthened the value that Goethe placed on tolerance in religious matters. Susanna von Klettenberg introduced him to the book by Gottfried Arnold (1666–1714), *History of the Church and Heretics* (1699–1700), which aimed to restore the reputations of mystical and unorthodox figures who had been condemned as heretics by the official Churches. For

Arnold, the Churches are tyrannical institutions, while the true followers of Jesus are the small number of genuinely spiritual people who follow their inner light and oppose priestly authority as Jesus did. Arnold therefore urges that all religious conviction should be tolerated, however unorthodox. He even has a good word to say for Muhammad, who in 18th-century Europe was still generally execrated.

Goethe put the case for tolerance in an attractive short text, *Letter from the Pastor at *** to the New Pastor at **** (1773). The old clergyman who writes a friendly letter to a newly appointed colleague is a lovable figure, but not a very plausible one, nor a mere mouthpiece for Goethe's views. Apparently a simple man, he has read not only the theologians but also Voltaire and Rousseau. He readily admits that parts of the Bible are unintelligible, and other parts boring. He rejects the doctrine of original sin. His central belief is in the love of God. God's love is so unfathomable that we cannot set bounds to it: we cannot say, for example, that it is denied to the heathen, though his parishioners unfortunately enjoy imagining that unbelievers will be roasted. The clergyman expects to meet the heathen in heaven: 'What joy it is to think that the Turk who considers me a dog, and the Jew who considers me a pig, will one day be glad to be my brothers.' He therefore advocates tolerance, insisting that tolerance of religion does not mean indifference to religion, as the orthodox claim. Indeed, 'when you look at things in the light, each person has his own religion'.

Goethe liked people who had a sincere, individual religious faith. His devout friends included the Pietist schoolteacher Heinrich Jung (1740–1817; known as Jung-Stilling) whose autobiography contains a memorable portrait of the young Goethe, and the Swiss clergyman Johann Caspar Lavater (1741–1801). But he also saw their faults. Lavater especially was led by his enthusiasm into intolerance: he told Goethe that if he was not a Christian he must be an atheist. In the poem 'Dinner at Coblenz', Goethe describes his position between two prophets, Lavater and the equally enthusiastic educationalist Basedow: 'prophets to my right, prophets to my left, and the child of this world in the middle'. His worry about self-styled prophets found expression in a drama about Muhammad, which he planned but did not complete. In contrast to the common 18th-century view of Muhammad as an impostor, Goethe would have depicted him as a truly devout and noble character whose zeal to propagate his religion led him into violence and deceit. We can detect here the lasting influence of Gottfried Arnold's sympathetic account of Muhammad, and also of Arnold's condemnation of institutional religion.

His friendship with Lavater helped Goethe to define his own religious position. In a letter of 29 July 1782, he told Lavater that he was 'zwar kein Widerkrist, kein Unkrist aber doch ein dezidierter Nichtkrist'. That is: he was not a Voltairean mocker of religion ('Widerkrist'), not an immoral person ('Unkrist'), but simply outside Christianity. He believed in God; but his God was that of Spinoza, who, as we have seen, was immanent in the world, not separate from the world. In addition, Goethe drew on Lucretius, whose poem *De rerum natura* (*On the Nature of the Universe*) set out a materialist understanding of the world and was read eagerly in the Enlightenment. There are different kinds of materialism, though. Goethe disliked the mechanical materialism of such French Enlightenment works as D'Holbach's *System of Nature* (1770) which presented a lifeless universe in a 'gloomy, atheistic semi-darkness'. In Lucretius' poem he found a material universe animated by desire, which the poet symbolizes by the figure of Venus, goddess of love. 'For my part,' he told the later Catholic convert Friedrich Stolberg in a letter of 2 February 1789, 'I am more or less attached to the doctrine of Lucretius.'

Goethe's standpoint was what the 18th century called 'natural religion'. He told Lavater firmly: 'You consider the Gospel the most divine truth; even a loud voice from heaven wouldn't convince *me* that water burns and fire puts it out, that a woman bears a child without a man, or that a man can rise from the dead; instead, I consider these beliefs to be blasphemies against the great God and his revelation in nature'. He thought it self-evident that there was a God who was manifested in the order of nature. Natural religion therefore did not require any effort of faith; it was only particular religions that did so. Natural religion sprang from 'the dialogue in our bosom with nature'; it depended on feeling and could not be implanted by rational argument. Hence what Faust professes to Gretchen is natural religion.

Iphigenie in Tauris

Goethe's allegiance to the Enlightenment emerges particularly in some texts which use classical mythology to pit humanity against the gods. The most aggressive of these is the poem 'Prometheus' (1774), uttered by the Titan who created humanity and stole fire from heaven in order to benefit his creatures. Prometheus defies Zeus, ridiculing his childish play with thunderbolts and asserting that the gods owe their power only to the credulity of childish mortals.

Very different in tone, but surprisingly similar in substance, is the neoclassical drama *Iphigenie in Tauris*. Goethe first wrote it in prose in 1779 and revised it in blank verse while in Italy in 1786–7. It is based on the ancient Greek play by Euripides, but with significant differences.

The play turns on the curse which afflicts all the family of Tantalus. Admitted to friendship with the gods, Tantalus overstepped the mark; as punishment, his descendants are doomed to mutual bloodshed. When one of them, Agamemnon, wanted to lead his fleet to the war against Troy, he was told that he could only obtain a fair wind if he sacrificed his daughter Iphigenie. Ten years later, returning from Troy, he was murdered by his unfaithful wife. Their son Orest was obliged to avenge his father by killing his mother. This was both a duty and a crime—a tragic dilemma imposed by the gods. Pursued by the Furies, he has learnt from the oracle of

Apollo that he can only be released if he brings home 'the sister' from the remote land of Tauris (the present-day Crimea), where a statue of Apollo's sister Artemis is kept.

However, the curse is not so easily undone. Iphigenie was saved by Artemis from her sacrificial death, and for the past ten years has served as priestess at the shrine of Artemis in Tauris. There she has weaned the populace from their custom of human sacrifice, and gained the affection of King Thoas. Annoyed by her refusal to marry him, however, Thoas threatens to restore sacrifices, and on learning that two Greeks have arrived on the coast, declares that Iphigenie as priestess must put them to death. When she learns that Orest is her brother, Iphigenie fears that the gods have contrived yet another cruel dilemma and that her family are doomed to go on murdering one another.

At this low point, half way through the play, matters start to improve. Orest is already in a state of near-suicidal depression; the prospect of being slaughtered by his sister sends him into a kind of trance, a near-death experience, from which he emerges restored to health and vigour. Many commentators ascribe his recovery to the healing influence exerted by Iphigenie. But since she is offstage when it happens, this can hardly be correct. Rather, it seems that Orest undergoes a natural process of crisis and regeneration, like Faust after the death of Gretchen and Wilhelm Meister after the disappearance of Mariane. And since the Furies, unlike in Euripides' play, never actually appear, we may interpret them as a metaphor for Orest's psychological distress and perhaps also as an analogy to the Christian conscience. Similarly, in *Faust I*, Gretchen at church is assailed by an Evil Spirit, representing her conscience, which sadistically warns her that God will damn her for her sin—though the Voice from Above, which finally declares that she is saved, shows how far orthodox Christians are from understanding God. The terrors of religion, in Goethe's view, do not make people better; they merely make them miserable, and one should instead trust to the healing powers of nature.

Once Orest is healed, all three Greeks plan to escape from Tauris. Iphigenie is to find a pretext for postponing the sacrifice, get down to the shore, and join the others on their ship. About this plan, however, she has two misgivings. One is that it requires her to deceive Thoas, although her innate integrity makes her find lying deeply repugnant; she fears it may even bring the Furies back as punishment. The other is that the escape plan has been thought up by two men, and Iphigenie is not best pleased at having to obey their orders like a child. Already in her opening monologue she has lamented that the condition of women is deplorable: subjection to a husband is bad enough, but as a solitary and homesick exile she has not even a husband's protection.

Although Iphigenie's moral scruples annoy Orest's companion Pylades, who cannot see why she should make a fuss about something so simple as lying, they in fact save the day. Unable to lie to Thoas—when she tries, her command of blank verse breaks down—she resolves instead to take the risk of telling him the truth. After all, she reasons with herself, men may display physical courage, but women can show moral courage, which is every bit as difficult. So she confesses to Thoas that her brother has arrived, with orders to steal the statue of Artemis. Though it is not easy to win Thoas round, he eventually agrees to let Iphigenie depart. Understandably, however, he baulks at losing the statue. But here Orest provides a solution. The oracle told him to bring 'the sister' back from Tauris; not knowing that Iphigenie was in Tauris, he naturally assumed that Apollo's sister was meant; but now it is clear that the oracle was referring to his own sister. Her return to Greece will finally dissolve the curse that has afflicted the house of Tantalus.

How do the gods come out of this? Their oracle was ambiguous, and it took human ingenuity to solve the riddle. But the gods do worse than give human beings futile puzzles. They set the curse in motion when they punished Tantalus for an unspecified offence which Iphigenie declares was merely human. She criticizes the gods by saying: 'Gods should not deal with humans as though with beings like themselves' (lines 315–16). The gods lead humanity into wrongdoing, then punish not only the malefactor but also his remote descendants. Again, analogies with Christianity suggest themselves: the God of the Old Testament proclaims himself to be 'a jealous God, visiting the iniquity of the fathers upon the children, upon the third and upon the fourth generation of them, that hate me' (Exodus 20: 5). Goethe claims that even as a child, hearing of the destruction of Lisbon by a tsunami, he reflected that the Father in Heaven had 'shown Himself by no means fatherly when he left the just and the unjust to perish alike'.

Fortunately, however, the gods seem to have only a poetic existence. While in Euripides the goddess Artemis appeared in person to resolve the plot, in Goethe neither the gods nor the Furies have any real, external existence. Iphigenie asserts that the gods speak to us through our hearts, and that those who think the gods bloodthirsty merely project their own cruelty on to them; but her own devout view of the gods (which she has some difficulty in sustaining) is equally a projection of her own honest and pure character. In Goethe's play, the gods have been superseded by humanity, religion by humanism. Iphigenie's continued references to 'the gods' imply no more than the natural religion to which Goethe was attached.

The humanist values expressed in the play are clearly better than those of religious cults. Both Greeks and barbarians look back with horror on a past history of bloody sacrifices. The Taurians are pleased to have abolished sacrifices under Iphigenie's influence. The play undermines the distinction, prominent in Euripides, between civilized Greeks and savage barbarians, by showing that both are struggling out of a brutal past and listening to 'the voice of truth and humanity'. In the spirit of Enlightenment cosmopolitanism, Iphigenie declares that this voice is audible 'To everyone, born under every sky, | Provided only that the spring of life | Runs pure and unobstructed through their bosom' (lines 1937–41). Nobody is excluded. Iphigenie's dangerous tactic of truth-telling opens up a new moral world, superior to the Machiavellian deceit that Pylades favours and to the violence to which Orest resorts. Finally, Iphigenie declares that in future visitors from Tauris will be welcome in Greece; and at the very end, she and Thoas shake hands—a gesture of human solidarity between equals, very different from kneeling before a god.

Beyond good and evil

Iphigenie is a compelling manifesto for a humanism compatible with natural religion. Elsewhere, however, natural religion, as Goethe develops it, reveals some troubling implications. One of these is slipped discreetly into the letter from the enlightened Pastor. The Pastor likes his Church's doctrine that faith, not works, is the prerequisite for salvation: 'This shows how much God loves us, for we can't do anything about Original Sin, nor about real sin, which is as natural as walking when you have feet'. That is, one cannot live without sinning, for sinning, like walking, just results from using one's natural (and God-given) faculties. But if sin is natural and inevitable, it ceases to be distinguishable from virtue. And if God and nature are the same, then virtue and sin, moral good and evil, no longer have a place in how we understand the world and how we live our lives.

Goethe consistently holds to this idea. In his Shakespeare lecture of 1771, where Shakespeare is praised as the poet closest to nature, Goethe concludes: 'What noble philosophers have often said about the world applies also to Shakespeare: what we call evil is only the other side of good [and] is as necessary for its existence and a part of the whole, as that the torrid zone must burn and Lapland freeze so that there is a temperate region.' He told his friend Sulpiz Boisserée that nature was 'an organ on which our Lord plays and the Devil treads the bellows' (8 September 1815).

Goethe seems to anticipate Nietzsche in viewing human life as 'beyond good and evil'. Throughout his life he rejected the Christian doctrine that human nature was inherently sinful. The Pietists with whom he consorted in his youth accused him of Pelagianism—that is, of siding with the early Christian heretic Pelagius who maintained that humanity was intrinsically good, in opposition to the grim doctrine of original sin put forward by his antagonist Augustine. A modern version of original sin, Kant's theory of radical evil, annoyed Goethe even more. In *Religion within the Bounds of Reason Alone* (1793), Kant cites ample evidence that human beings are naturally bad, ranging from our secret satisfaction in our friends' misfortunes to the gratuitous cruelty attributed to native Americans. Goethe refused to believe in this innate propensity to evil. He charged Kant with 'defiling his philosophical robe with the shameful stain of radical evil' in order to ingratiate himself with Christians (letter to the Herders, 7 June 1793). As we have seen, Goethe's heroes incur guilt, but their guilt is treated less as a moral problem than as a medical issue, to be overcome by the healing power of nature.

Rejecting both original sin and radical evil, Goethe was certainly no Augustinian. But it is not clear that he was a Pelagian, either. His supreme heroes—the fictional Faust, the historical Napoleon—are forces of nature, 'daemonic' in the sense described earlier. The destruction they wreak certainly qualifies their greatness, but does not annul it. Faust is directly responsible for the death of Gretchen, indirectly responsible for that of Philemon and Baucis, yet neither crime prevents his admission to heaven.

What matters to Goethe is individuality. In life and literature, he likes people who have strong, distinct personalities, who are genuine, spontaneous, natural, and who seek to realize their individuality. It is because Faust never abandons this endeavour, despite Mephisto's efforts to distract him, that he is saved: 'He who strives on and lives to strive | Can earn redemption still' (lines 11936–7). In the *Divan*, Zuleika asserts:

> Volk und Knecht und Überwinder
> Sie gestehn, zu jeder Zeit,

Höchstes Glück der Erdenkinder
Sei nur die Persönlichkeit.

People, vassal and conqueror, all admit in every age: the supreme happiness of earth's children is personality.

Near the end of his life, in the posthumously published essay 'One more Word for Young Poets', Goethe said that for young poets he had been a liberator, 'for they saw from my example that, just as a person must live from the inside outwards, so the artist must have his effect from the inside outwards, since, whatever he does, he will always bring forth only his individuality.'

Goethe's stress on individuality brings him close to the greatest contemporary philosopher, Kant. Kant's injunction in 'What is Enlightenment?' to think for oneself, without blindly obeying external authorities, matched Goethe's outlook; Iphigenie, acting independently of her male companions and following her own moral intuitions, puts it into practice. Beyond that, just how much Goethe owed to Kant is disputed. His essay 'Influence of Recent Philosophy' (1817) begins with the disarming admission that he has no aptitude for philosophy on the strict sense, and makes clear that it cost him a struggle to make sense of the *Critique of Pure Reason* (1781); the *Critique of Judgement* (1790), which deals partly with aesthetics, was more congenial. Schiller thought that Goethe understood Kant in too subjective a manner, taking from the latter's works what he wanted to find there. Even so, there are strong echoes of Kant in the late poem to which Goethe gave the portentous title 'Vermächtnis' ('Legacy', 1829), especially in the lines:

Denn das selbstständige Gewissen
Ist Sonne deinem Sittentag.

For the independent conscience is the sun to your moral day.

The combination of astronomical and ethical language here recalls Kant's famous conclusion in the *Critique of Practical*

Reason (1788): 'Two things fill the heart with ever renewed and increasing admiration and awe, the more one thinks about them: the starry sky above me, and the moral law in me.' But by speaking of the 'independent' conscience, the poem adds an individual, Goethean twist. For while Kant assumes that one will recognize a pre-existing moral law, the Goethean conscience, in being independent, is capable of creating new values, as Iphigenie does when she moves beyond the conventional antithesis of Greek and barbarian. When Goethe read philosophy, he did not passively accept it, but entered into a critical and very personal dialogue with it.

Earthly life

If Goethe anticipates Nietzsche in envisioning an existence beyond good and evil, he does so also by proclaiming the supreme value of earthly life. Nietzsche's prophet in *Thus Spoke Zarathustra* (1883) tells his hearers: 'I beseech you, my brothers, *stay true to the earth* and do not believe those who talk of over-earthly hopes!' Goethe deplored the Christian asceticism which dwells on the suffering and misery of earthly life and announces a compensatory afterlife in heaven. He especially disliked images of the martyred Christ. The speaker in 'The Diary' confesses that on his wedding day in church, despite the presence of the cross, he had an erection—an affirmation of life against what Goethe perceived as a cult of death. In Verona in 1786, Goethe admired ancient funerary monuments which depicted figures with natural emotions:

> And the grave monuments are warm and touching. You see a man beside his wife looking out of a niche as if from a window, a father and mother stand with their son between them and look at one another with ineffable naturalness, a couple stretch out their hands to each other.... I was so deeply moved in the presence of these stones that I could not hold back my tears. Here is no man in armour on his knees waiting for a joyous resurrection, what the

> artist has here set down with more or less skill is never anything more than the simple present of human beings, which thereby prolongs their existence and makes it permanent.

Goethe's thoughts on how to incorporate religious feeling into an existence firmly focused on this world find expression in his late novel, *Wilhelm Meisters Wanderjahre* (*Wilhelm Meister's Journeyman Years*). First published in 1823 and then in enlarged form in 1829, this text will disconcert anyone who expects a simple sequel to *Wilhelm Meister's Apprenticeship*. The characters are little more than names; the rudimentary plot is interrupted by aphorisms, inset novellas, mini-essays, and even a detailed account of cotton-weaving. The Society of the Tower have now transformed themselves into the League of Emigrants and plan to found a colony in America, where Wilhelm, now training as a surgeon, will join them. These materials are held together by intricate symbolism; but the symbols are *only* symbols. Goethe's aesthetic requires the artist to imitate the world of the senses vividly, so that the symbolic meaning will be a bonus; but in this late novel the task of imitating nature has been elbowed aside by Goethe's didactic purposes.

While still in Europe, Wilhelm places his son Felix in a strange educational institution called the Pedagogical Province. The religious instruction here consists in teaching children a threefold reverence: for what is above us (the sky, God), for what is beneath us (the earth), and for what is on our own level (our fellow-humans). This threefold reverence combines what is valuable in paganism and in Christianity, accepting even sin and crime as aids to the better appreciation of the sacred. Accordingly, the Province has a gallery with pictures illustrating scenes from Greek mythology and from the Old and New Testaments, but it contains no picture of Christ's crucifixion, for they consider it an impertinence to put something so deeply serious on public display (an implied rebuke to standard Christian iconography). The Province does not reject Christianity, but seeks to purify it from what might be considered disgusting or absurd, and to incorporate it into a higher, synthetic religion.

The novel shows Goethe's concern for practical activity, for which it adapts the term *Frömmigkeit* (piety). This word usually implies the regular and dutiful service of God; Goethe first coins the term *Hausfrömmigkeit*, suggesting an equally devout service directed to sustaining one's household and family, and then extends it further by making a character say: 'we need to form the concept of a world piety (*Weltfrömmigkeit*), to create a practical link between our decent human disposition and the wider world, and help not only our neighbour, but also the whole of humanity' (II, 7). Thus we have a religious outlook which is practical rather than contemplative, which sees *doing* good as the best way of *being* good, and which, in the spirit of Enlightenment cosmopolitanism, concerns itself not just with one's narrow family circle but with humanity as a whole.

Interpreters of the *Journeyman Years* have often been influenced by its subtitle, *oder Die Entsagenden* ('or Those who renounce, who practise self-denial'). The late Goethe has been charged with a gloomy outlook. Certainly Goethe was no shallow optimist. He told Eckermann on 27 January 1824 that though he had had in many ways a fortunate life, it had involved continual toil and labour: 'I may well say that in my seventy-five years I have not known four weeks of actual ease.' In his autobiography he insists that all experience tells us that we must practise renunciation: that is, we must accept disappointment, frustration, the unlived life; nevertheless, it would be false and even blasphemous to declare that 'all is vanity', and the highest, most difficult wisdom consists in calmly resigning ourselves to the necessary course of earthly life. By this standard, the renunciation practised in the *Journeyman Years* is minor. Wilhelm is separated for some years from Natalie, but it is clear that he will rejoin her in America. Earlier characters in Goethe's fiction have practised renunciation: Lotte renounces Werther after their one passionate embrace,

Charlotte in *Elective Affinities* conquers her feelings for the Captain; but in these cases Goethe shows us the painful effort required by such self-sacrifice, whereas in the *Journeyman Years* renunciation is merely a word.

In any case, Goethe was rarely if ever tempted to reject the world. A great poem of 1803, 'Dauer im Wechsel' ('Permanence in Change'), appears to lament the transience of life: blossoms on a tree are soon dispersed by the wind, every shower of rain alters the shape of a valley, and (quoting the Greek philosopher Heraclitus) you cannot swim in the same river twice. But the tremendous energy that powers the poem undoes the appearance of melancholy and conveys instead an immense gusto in the act of living. Similarly, almost thirty years later, the poem 'Legacy', already quoted, invites us to enjoy life, albeit in sensible moderation, and thus retain the past, look forward to the future, and endow the passing moment with an intensity that takes it out of time: 'the moment is eternity'.

And afterwards? Despite his focus on earthly life, Goethe was intuitively convinced that the individual must survive after death. He thought it a waste of time to speculate on the form this survival might take, but he hoped it would be active, as he could not stand idleness. Occasionally, as we have seen from the poems 'Why did you give us deep insight' and 'Blessed Yearning', he found at least imaginative appeal in the doctrine of transmigration of souls. His longest and strangest reflections on continued existence, however, were prompted by an event that grieved him deeply, the death of the great Enlightenment writer Christoph Martin Wieland in January 1813. It was inconceivable, he told his Weimar friend J. D. Falk, that such a lofty soul as Wieland's could simply perish. To explain how it might survive, he referred to Leibniz's concept of the monad, that is, the inner core or essential energies of an individual being. Just as a plant retains its identity through all its metamorphoses, or a caterpillar remains the same being when it has becomes a butterfly, so a person's monad may retain its identity when passing through stages which at present we cannot imagine.

The conversation with Falk helps us to understand Faust's ascent to heaven in the last scene of *Faust II*. Faust's 'immortal part', which the angels save from Mephisto's clutches, may be understood as his monad, or, in a term that Goethe derived ultimately from Aristotle and used in a similar sense, his entelechy or essence. The Faust who appears in this scene does not speak. He is no longer the earthly individual who has passed through so many adventures in the play; he is described as being in a 'chrysalis' (line 11982), gradually shedding his earthly coverings, to emerge as a new being. This may be read as the ultimate poetic expression of Goethe's intuitive confidence in the healing and transformative powers of divinely animated nature—what a poem inserted at the very end of the *Journeyman Years* calls 'Gott-Natur'.

A chronology of Goethe's life and works

1749	28 August: Johann Wolfgang Goethe born into a well-to-do family, Johann Kaspar Goethe and Katharina Elisabeth Goethe née Textor, in Frankfurt am Main.
1750–7	December: birth of his sister Cornelia.
1752–65	Goethe is privately educated. He has tutors in French, Hebrew, Italian, English.
1755	Lisbon earthquake.
1756–63	Seven Years' War.
1765–8	Studies law at the University of Leipzig. Early love affairs (Käthchen Schönkopf).
	August 1768–March 1770: mostly at home in Frankfurt, often ill. Associates with Pietists under the guidance of Susanna von Klettenberg.
1770–1	Studies in Strasbourg. Love-affair with Friederike Brion. Friendship with Herder. Reads Shakespeare, Ossian, Homer.
1771–4	Works as barrister in Frankfurt and Wetzlar.
1771	First version of *Götz von Berlichingen*.
1774	First version of *The Sorrows of Young Werther* published.
1775	Engaged to Lili Schönemann. Journey to Switzerland. Begins *Egmont*. Invited to Weimar as companion to the young Duke Carl August. Breaks off his engagement. Arrives in Weimar on 7 November.

1776	Becomes a member of the Privy Council which governs Weimar. Visits the silver mine at Ilmenau, which over the years he will try to reopen.
1776–86	Increasingly involved in administrative duties. Relationship with Charlotte von Stein. Works for the Weimar theatre; makes scientific studies, especially in geology; begins work on *Wilhelm Meister*, *Iphigenie in Tauris* (in prose), *Torquato Tasso*.
1777	8 June: death of his sister Cornelia. November and December: visits the Harz Mountains; climbs the Brocken.
1782	Ennobled with the predicate 'von'.
1786	Feeling confined in Weimar, and frustrated by his relationship with Charlotte von Stein, leaves secretly for Italy on 3 September. 29 October: arrives in Rome.
1786–8	Stays in Rome, Naples, Sicily, and Rome again. Much contact with artists and work of art. Completes *Egmont*. Revises *Iphigenie* in verse.
1788	18 June: back in Weimar. Relieved of most of his official duties. 12 July: begins relationship with Christiane Vulpius.
1789	Completes *Tasso*. 14 July: fall of the Bastille, beginning of French Revolution. 25 December: birth of August, the only child of Goethe and Christiane to survive.
1790	March–June: second Italian journey, this time to Venice. Partial publication of *Faust* as *Faust*: *A Fragment*.
1792	Accompanies Prussian forces to France and witnesses their defeat at the Battle of Valmy, 20 September.
1793	21 January: execution of Louis XVI. May–July: Goethe present at the siege of Mainz.
1794	Begins correspondence with Schiller, who lives in nearby Jena.

1795	*Roman Elegies* published in Schiller's journal *Die Horen* (*The Hours*).
1796	Publishes *Wilhelm Meister's Apprenticeship.*
1797	Publishes *Hermann and Dorothea.*
1799	Schiller moves to Weimar.
1803	Publishes *The Natural Daughter.*
1805	Death of Schiller.
1806	Goethe marries Christiane Vulpius.
	18 October: Battle of Jena, in which Napoleon's forces defeat Prussia. French troops enter Weimar and invade Goethe's house.
1808	2 and 6 October: meetings with Napoleon in Erfurt.
	Faust Part I published
1809	Publishes *Elective Affinities.*
1811	Begins work on his autobiography, *Poetry and Truth.*
1812	Napoleon's retreat from Moscow.
1814–18	Friendship with Marianne von Willemer; writes poems of the *West-Eastern Divan.*
1816	6 June: death of Christiane.
1816–17	Publishes the *Italian Journey.*
1821	Publishes first version of *Wilhelm Meister's Journeyman Years.*
1823–4	In love with Ulrike von Levetzow; writes the poems forming the 'Trilogie der Leidenschaft' ('Trilogy of Passion').
1823–32	Many conversations recorded by his secretary Johann Peter Eckermann.
1825–31	Continues work on *Faust II.*
1832	22 March: Goethe's death.

Publisher's acknowledgements

We are grateful for permission to include the following copyright material in this book.

Extracts from *The Sorrows of Young Werther*, by Johann Wolfgang von Goethe, edited by David Constantine (2012), by permission of Oxford University Press.

Extracts from *Elective Affinities: A Novel*, by J. W. von Goethe, translated by David Constantine, Oxford World's Classics (2008), by permission of Oxford University Press.

Extracts from *Goethe: The Flight to Italy*, by J. W. von Goethe, translated by T. J. Reed, Oxford World's Classics (1999), by permission of Oxford University Press.

Extracts from *Goethe: Faust part 1*, by J. W. von Goethe, translated by David Luke, Oxford World's Classics (2008), by permission of Oxford University Press.

Extracts from *Goethe: Faust part 2*, by J. W. von Goethe, translated by David Luke, Oxford World's Classics (2008), by permission of Oxford University Press.

Extracts from *Goethe: The Erotic Poems*, by J. W. von Goethe, translated by David Luke, Oxford World's Classics (2008), by permission of Libris.

The publisher and author have made every effort to trace and contact all copyright holders before publication. If notified, the publisher will be pleased to rectify any errors or omissions at the earliest opportunity.

References

To keep this section short, wherever possible sufficient references have been included in the text to enable the reader to find the quoted passage in either an English or a German edition. Quotations from *Werther* are identified by the date of Werther's letter; from *Elective Affinities* and *Wilhelm Meister's Apprenticeship*, by books and chapter number. Quotations from verse plays, including *Faust*, are identified by line number. As the *Italian Journey* is largely in diary form, quotations are identified by date. Letters are identified by date and recipient.

In his later years, several people took down Goethe's conversation. The most assiduous was Johann Peter Eckermann, who served as secretary during the last ten years of Goethe's life, and afterwards published three volumes of *Conversations with Goethe*. Eckermann's reliability has been questioned. He relied heavily on his memory. In one case he reconstructed a conversation, covering ten pages, fourteen years after the event, and on the basis of four words noted down at the time. Contemporaries agreed that he captured Goethe's style and tone perfectly. It is probably safe to assume that Eckermann's records are accurate in substance, but that he rarely if ever reported Goethe's exact words. These and other conversations are identified by date and interlocutor.

There are numerous editions of Goethe's works. Wherever possible, I have referred readers with German to the Frankfurt edition (abbreviated as FA with volume and page number): Johann Wolfgang Goethe, *Sämtliche Werke: Briefe, Tagebücher und Gespräche*, ed. Friedmar Apel and others, 40 vols. (Frankfurt a.M.: Deutscher Klassiker Verlag, 1986–2000). Occasionally I have cited the 19th-century Weimar edition (WA): *Goethes Werke*, hrsg. im Auftrage der Großherzogin Sophie von Sachsen, ed. Bernhard Suphan and others, IV sections, 143 vols. (Weimar: Böhlau, 1887–1919); and the Hamburg Edition (HA): Johann Wolfgang Goethe, *Werke*, ed. Erich Trunz, 14 vols. (Hamburg: Wegner, 1949–60).

Preface

'Goethe is the greatest poet': 'A French Critic on Goethe' in *The Complete Prose Works of Matthew Arnold*, ed. R. H. Super, 11 vols. (Ann Arbor: University of Michigan Press, 1960–77), vol. 8: *Essays Religious and Mixed*, 252–76 (275).

'But *is* it so?': 'Heinrich Heine' in ibid., vol. 3: *Lectures and Essays on Criticism*, 106–32 (110).

Chapter 1: Love

The Sufferings of Young Werther

'I know the book': Auguste, Countess Stolberg, quoted in HA vi. 524.

Werther as confession?

'fragments': FA xiv. 310.

'In Moments': FA i. 34.

'With my sister': letter to his mother, 16 Nov. 1777.

'This heart on fire'

'Willkommen und Abschied': FA i. 128, cf. 283.

'Das du so': FA i. 234, cf. 301. The plural 'you' is commonly thought to allude to Charlotte von Lassberg, who drowned herself with *Werther* in her pocket.

Rome, Christiane Vulpius, and the creaking bed

'Set in modern Rome': for the elegiac distich, see Judith Ryan, *The Cambridge Introduction to German Poetry* (Cambridge: Cambridge University Press, 2012), appendix.

'lofty poetic beauty': quoted in Hans Rudolf Vaget, 'Introduction', Johann Wolfgang von Goethe, *Erotic Poems*, tr. David Luke, Oxford World's Classics (Oxford: Oxford University Press, 1997), ix–xlix (xxi).

'She sweetly breathes': FA i. 406; *Erotic Poems*, 15.

'We make short work': FA i. 394; *Erotic Poems*, 7.

'Such a dear': Catharina Elisabeth Goethe, letter to her son, 17 Apr. 1807, in Goethe, *Briefe au dem Elternhaus*, ed. Ernst Beutler (Frankfurt a.M.: Insel, 1997), 850.

Sublimation

'Du beschämst': FA iii. 87–8.

'For life is love': FA iii. 88.

'Dem Frieden Gottes': FA ii. 460.

Chapter 2: Nature

'Goethe's conviction': see conversation with Riemer, 19 Mar. 1807.

'Auf dem See': FA i. 297.

'Goethe pointed to storms': FA xviii. 98.

'For Nature is unfeeling': FA i. 333.

'What sort of God': FA ii. 379.

'What we see of Nature': FA xviii. 99.

'these few words': letter to F.H. Jacobi, 5 May 1786.

'The eye': FA xiv. 246.

Goethe's study of nature

'how delightful': FA xv/1. 712; Goethe, *The Flight to Italy*, tr. T. J. Reed, Oxford World's Classics (Oxford: Oxford University Press, 1999), 86.

'universal monarchy': FA xiii. 167.

'seek with all': FA xxv. 114.

'The supreme goal': FA xxv. 114.

'What we become aware of': FA xxiii/1: 80–1.

'That isn't an experience': 'Glückliches Ereignis' (1817), FA xxv. 437.

'I have no more urgent task': to Wilhelm von Humboldt, 17 Mar. 1832.

'Much more has': FA xiii. 271.

'only the whole': letter to Schiller, 5 May 1798.

'in New York': FA xxv. 92.

Morphology

'And it would therefore be completely impossible': FA ii. 500.

Geology

'geological fantasies': letter of 31 Oct. 1840, quoted in Kurt-R. Biermann, 'Goethe in vertraulichen Briefen Alexander von Humboldts', *Goethe-Jahrbuch*, 102 (1985), 11–33 (20).

'That the Himalayas': letter to Zelter, 5 Oct. 1831.

The doctrine of colours

'If the eye': FA ii. 645.

'You know how': FA xv/1. 660; *The Flight to Italy*, 47.

Nature and literature: *Wilhelm Meister's Apprenticeship*

'bildende Kraft': FA xxiv. 280.

'Lied und Gebilde': FA iii. 21.

Chapter 3: Classical art and world literature

Goethe and visual art

'creative power': FA xiv. 837.

'Art should not': FA xviii. 731.

'Just as in the eternal works': FA xviii. 115.

'strong, rugged German soul': FA xviii. 117.

Classicism

'The more one studies': letter to J. H. Meyer, 30 Oct. 1795.

'Here we have a talent': 'Antik und modern', FA xx. 349.

The aesthetics of classicism

'Goethe once gloomily compared': letter to Schiller, 18 Mar. 1801.

'das Kunstwahre': 'Über Wahrheit und Wahrscheinlichkeit der Kunstwerke' (1798), FA xviii. 504; 'On Truth and Probability in Works of Art'.

'the connoisseur sees': ibid., FA xviii. 506.

'since he extracts': 'Einleitung zu den *Propyläen*', FA xviii. 465; 'Introduction to the *Propyläen*'.

'the beautiful proportions': ibid., FA xviii. 465.

'The *born artist*': 'Über die bildende Nachahmung des Schönen', FA xviii. 257.

'the artist, in the purity': 'Ruysdael als Dichter' (1816), FA xix. 636.

Classicism or Romanticism?

'neo-Catholic sentimentalism': 'Neu-deutsche religios-patriotische Kunst' (1817), written by Heinrich Meyer in consultation with Goethe, FA xx. 105–29.

World literature

'the incomparable Jones': 'Indische Dichtungen' (1821?), WA I, vol. 42/ii, 51.

'He wrote a quatrain': letter to F. H. Jacobi, 1 June 1791.

The *West-Eastern Divan*

'a second Voltaire': to Sulpiz Boisserée, Aug. 1815.

Chapter 4: Politics

The Holy Roman Empire

'He professed': letter to Johann Caspar Lavater, 9 Aug. 1782.

Weimar

'state murder': quoted in W. Daniel Wilson, *Das Goethe-Tabu: Protest und Menschenrechte im klassischen Weimar* (Munich: dtv, 1999), 8.

The French Revolution

'the most dreadful': 'Bedeutende Fördernis durch ein einziges geistreiches Wort' (1823), FA xxiv. 597.

'Here begins': *Campagne in Frankreich* (1822), FA xvi. 436.

'In the end': *Belagerung von Mainz* (1820), FA xvi. 603.

'scandalous law': to Kanzler von Müller, 23 Sept. 1823.

Politics in literature

'What is the freest man': FA v. 525.

'A good citizen': FA v. 486–7.

'stand firm': FA v. 487.

'After the vision': George Santayana, *Three Philosophical Poets: Lucretius, Dante, Goethe* (Cambridge, MA: Harvard University Press, 1910), 182.

'that development': Karl Marx, *Selected Writings*, ed. David McLellan (Oxford: Oxford University Press, 1977), 497.

'the tragedy of the developer': Marshall Berman, *All that is Solid Melts into Air: The Experience of Modernity* (London: Verso, 1983), 66.

Napoleon and the daemonic

'the highest phenomenon': letter to Knebel, 3 Jan. 1807.

'a power': FA xiv. 841.

'Extraordinary people': to Riemer, 3 Feb. 1807.
'Übermacht': FA iii. 54.

Chapter 5: Tragedy

Modern tragedy

'broad and ugly ditch': 'On the Proof of the Spirit and of Power' in Lessing, *Philosophical and Theological Writings*, tr. H. B. Nisbet (Cambridge: Cambridge University Press, 2005), 87.

Chapter 6: Religion

Goethe and the Enlightenment

'Poetic Thoughts': FA i. 17–21.
'the rugged naturalness': FA xiv. 556.
'What joy': FA xviii. 123.
'prophets to right and left': FA i. 164 (where this section is considered a separate poem).
'gloomy, atheistic semi-darkness': FA xiv. 535.
'You consider': letter to Lavater, 9 Aug. 1782.
'the dialogue': FA xiv. 245.

Iphigenie in Tauris

'shown Himself': FA xiv. 37.

Beyond good and evil

'This shows how much': FA xviii. 121.
'What noble philosophers': FA xviii. 12.
'Volk und Knecht': FA iii. 84.
'for they saw from my example': FA xxii. 933.
'Denn das': FA ii. 685.

Earthly life

'I beseech you': Friedrich Nietzsche, *Thus Spoke Zarathustra*, tr. Graham Parkes, Oxford World's Classics (Oxford: Oxford University Press, 2005), 12.
'And the grave monuments': FA xv/1. 645; *The Flight to Italy*, 34–5.
'all experience tells us': FA xiv. 729.
'Dauer im Wechsel': FA ii. 78–9.
'the moment is eternity': FA ii. 686.
'Gott-Natur': FA ii. 685, x. 774.

Translations and further reading

Translations

Goethe's major works are available in translations of generally high quality as *Collected Works*, 12 vols. (Princeton: Princeton University Press, 1995), including a large selection from his scientific writings.

Generous selections of Goethe's poetry have been translated in prose by David Luke in *Goethe*, The Penguin Poets (Harmondsworth: Penguin, 1964), reissued as a bilingual edition, and in verse by John Whaley in *Goethe: Selected Poems* (London: Dent, 1998). Whaley has also made a complete bilingual edition of the *Divan* as *Poems of the West and the East* (Bern: Peter Lang, 1998). David Luke has provided a parallel text of the *Erotic Poems* (Oxford World's Classics, 1988), comprising the uncut *Roman Elegies*, *The Diary*, and some shorter pieces.

Translations of *Faust* are innumerable. Those by David Luke (Oxford World's Classics, 1987 and 1998) can be particularly recommended. In addition to the versions in the *Collected Works* (above), *Egmont* has been translated by Francis Lamport in *Five German Tragedies* (Harmondsworth: Penguin, 1969), *Tasso* by Alan Brownjohn (London: Angel Books, 1985), while a slightly abridged version of *Iphigenie* by Roy Pascal, originally broadcast in 1954, was published by Angel Books in 2014.

There are translations of *Werther* by Michael Hulse (Penguin, 1989) and David Constantine (Oxford World's Classics, 2012); of *Elective*

Affinities by R. J. Hollingdale (Penguin, 1971) and David Constantine (Oxford World's Classics, 1994). The most recent translation of *Wilhelm Meister's Apprenticeship* is by Eric Blackall in the *Collected Works*; a new translation by Jeremy Adler is in preparation.

The *Italian Journey* was translated by W. H. Auden and Elizabeth Mayer (Penguin, 1970). The diary of Goethe's first few months in Italy, which formed the basis of the later and more sedate narrative, has been translated by T. J. Reed as *The Flight to Italy* (Oxford World's Classics, 1999). For Goethe's art criticism, see *Goethe on Art*, ed. and tr. John Gage (Berkeley and Los Angeles: University of California Press, 1980).

Further reading

This list is confined to studies in English. The best starting-point is John R. Williams, *The Life of Goethe* (Oxford: Blackwell, 1998), which provides not only a biography but also concise and expert introductions to Goethe's works. More detailed is the magisterial and often absorbing biography by Nicholas Boyle, *Goethe: The Poet and the Age*, vol. 1: *The Poetry of Desire*; vol. 2: *Revolution and Renunciation*, 1790–1803 (Oxford: Clarendon Press, 1991 and 2000); a third volume is awaited. Barker Fairley, *A Study of Goethe* (Oxford: Clarendon Press, 1947), is a vivid account of Goethe's works and his personality. T. J. Reed, *Goethe*, Past Masters (Oxford: Oxford University Press, 1984) is an introduction on the same scale as the present one but with a somewhat different approach. Excellent introductions to a range of topics are provided in Lesley Sharpe (ed.), *The Cambridge Companion to Goethe* (Cambridge: Cambridge University Press, 2002).

Chapter 1: Love

A detailed introduction to *Werther* is Martin Swales, *Goethe, 'The Sorrows of Young Werther'* (Cambridge: Cambridge University Press, 1987). On its impact, see Stuart Atkins, *The Testament of Werther in Poetry and Drama* (Cambridge, MA: Harvard University Press, 1949).

On *Elective Affinities*, see the stimulating chapter in Tony Tanner, *Adultery in the Novel* (Baltimore: Johns Hopkins University Press, 1979), 179–232, and some important articles: H. B. Nisbet, '*Die Wahlverwandtschaften*: Explanation and its Limits', *Deutsche*

Vierteljahresschrift, 43 (1969), 458–86; Ronald Peacock, 'The Ethics of Goethe's *Die Wahlverwandtschaften*', *Modern Language Review*, 71 (1976), 330–43; Karl Leydecker, 'The Avoidance of Divorce in Goethe's *Die Wahlverwandtschaften*', *Modern Language Review*, 106 (2011), 1054–72. A guide to these and Goethe's other novels is Eric A. Blackall, *Goethe and the Novel* (Ithaca, NY: Cornell University Press, 1976).

For introductions to Goethe's poetry, see Barker Fairley, *Goethe as Revealed in his Poetry* (London: Dent, 1932); T. J. Reed (ed.), Goethe, *Selected Poems* (London: Bristol Classical Press, 1999)—poems in German, but introduction and commentary in English.

On the relations between the mind and the body, see Matthew Bell, *Goethe's Naturalistic Anthropology: Man and Other Plants* (Oxford: Clarendon Press, 1994), which includes a study of *Werther*.

Chapter 2: Nature

For Goethe's place in scientific thought I have relied particularly on H. B. Nisbet, *Goethe and the Scientific Tradition* (London: Institute of Germanic Studies, 1972), and G. A. Wells, *Goethe and the Development of Science, 1750–1900* (Alphen aan den Rijn: Sijthoff & Noordhoff, 1978). More positive accounts of Goethe's science are given by Astrida Orle Tantillo, *The Will to Create: Goethe's Philosophy of Nature* (Pittsburgh: University of Pittsburgh Press, 2002), Robert Richards, *The Romantic Conception of Life: Science and Philosophy in the Age of Goethe* (Chicago: University of Chicago Press, 2002), and Daniel Steuer in his contribution to the *Cambridge Companion*. E. M. Wilkinson, long the doyenne of Goethe studies, interprets Goethe's literary works in relation to his science in her book written jointly with L. A. Willoughby, *Goethe: Poet and Thinker* (London: Arnold, 1962). The doctrine of colours is minutely examined by Dennis L. Sepper, *Goethe contra Newton: Polemics and the Project for a New Science of Color* (Cambridge: Cambridge University Press, 1988).

On *Wilhelm Meister's Apprenticeship*, see especially Michael Beddow, *The Fiction of Humanity* (Cambridge: Cambridge University Press, 1982), ch. 2. David Roberts, *The Indirections of Desire: Hamlet in Goethe's 'Wilhelm Meister'* (Heidelberg: Winter, 1980), and Michael Minden, *The German Bildungsroman: Incest and Inheritance*

(Cambridge: Cambridge University Press, 1997), ch. 1, offer psychoanalytic approaches. On its character as the exemplary 'Bildungsroman', see James Hardin (ed.), *Reflection and Action: Essays in the Bildungsroman* (Columbia, SC: University of South Carolina Press, 1991). For its place in European literature, see Franco Moretti, *The Way of the World: The 'Bildungsroman' in European Culture* (London: Verso, 1987).

Chapter 3: Classical art and world literature

The art historian John Gage has performed a great service by translating a generous selection of Goethe's writings on art, with a short but useful introduction, as *Goethe on Art* (Berkeley and Los Angeles: University of California Press, 1980). W. D. Robson-Scott, *The Younger Goethe and the Visual Arts* (Cambridge: Cambridge University Press, 1981), is fascinating. On Goethe's conception of world literature and its background, see John Pizer, 'Cosmopolitanism and Weltliteratur', *Goethe Yearbook*, 13 (2005), 165–79, and Ritchie Robertson, '*Weltliteratur* from Voltaire to Goethe', *Comparative Critical Studies*, 12 (2015), 163–81.

Chapter 4: Politics

On Goethe's Germany, two studies by W. H. Bruford, *Germany in the Eighteenth Century* (Cambridge: Cambridge University Press, 1935) and *Culture and Society in Classical Weimar 1775–1806* (Cambridge: Cambridge University Press, 1962), remain indispensable. Standard accounts of the Holy Roman Empire as moribund have recently been challenged by Joachim Whaley, *Germany and the Holy Roman Empire* (Oxford: Oxford University Press, 2012).

The extent of Goethe's conservatism as an administrator has been revealed in numerous studies by W. Daniel Wilson, based on research in the Weimar archives, and summarized in his essay 'Goethe and the Political World' in the *Cambridge Companion*. He has reconstructed the story of Johanna Höhn's execution in 'Goethe, his Duke and Infanticide: New Documents and Reflections on a Controversial Execution', *German Life and Letters*, 61 (2008), 7–32. On the 'daemonic' and its intellectual sources, see Angus Nicholls, *Goethe's Concept of the Daemonic: After the Ancients* (Rochester, NY: Camden House, 2006). Among many essays on Goethe as political dramatist, see especially F. J. Lamport, '"Entfernten Weltgetöses Widerhall":

Politics in Goethe's Plays', *Publications of the English Goethe Society*, 44 (1973–4), 41–62, and W. Daniel Wilson, 'Hunger/Artist: Goethe's Revolutionary Agitators in *Götz, Satyros, Egmont* and *Der Bürgergeneral*', *Monatshefte*, 86 (1994), 80–94.

Chapter 5: Tragedy

My approach to tragedy in general follows Terry Eagleton, *Sweet Violence: The Idea of the Tragic* (Oxford: Blackwell, 2003), and some passages in C. S. Lewis, *An Experiment in Criticism* (Cambridge: Cambridge University Press, 1961). Erich Heller's essay 'Goethe and the Avoidance of Tragedy' in his *The Disinherited Mind* (Cambridge: Bowes & Bowes, 1952), 29–49, remains useful to argue with. A different account of the late Goethe's understanding of tragedy is offered by Nicholas Boyle, 'Goethe's Theory of Tragedy', *Modern Language Review*, 105 (2010), 1072–86.

Commentary on *Faust* is huge. Useful guides include: John R. Williams, *Goethe's 'Faust'* (London: Allen & Unwin, 1987); Nicholas Boyle, *Goethe: 'Faust I'* (Cambridge: Cambridge University Press, 1987); Barker Fairley, *Goethe's 'Faust': Six Essays* (Oxford: Clarendon Press, 1953); and Paul Bishop (ed.), *A Companion to Goethe's 'Faust': Parts I and II* (Rochester, NY: Camden House, 2001). Eudo C. Mason, *Goethe's 'Faust': Its Genesis and Purport* (Berkeley and Los Angeles: University of California Press, 1967), is a deeply searching study which attends especially to Goethe's conceptions of good and evil. An imaginative, wide-ranging study, informed but not dominated by psychoanalysis, is James Simpson, *Goethe and Patriarchy: Faust and the Fates of Desire* (Oxford: Legenda, 1998). On *Faust* and its afterlife (rewritings, films, rock musicals), see Osman Durrani, *Faust: Icon of Modern Culture* (Robertsbridge: Helm Information, 2004). Challenging new readings of *Faust* and *Tasso* are offered in K. F. Hilliard, *Freethinkers, Libertines and 'Schwärmer': Heterodoxy in German Literature* (London: Institute of Germanic & Romance Studies, 2011).

Chapter 6: Religion

For Goethe's principles of religious toleration, see the wide-ranging study by Paul E. Kerry, *Enlightenment Thought in the Writings of Goethe: A Contribution to the History of Ideas* (Rochester, NY: Camden House, 2001). On Goethe's contribution to the Enlightenment more generally, see T. J. Reed, *Light in Germany: Scenes from an Unknown Enlightenment* (Chicago: University of Chicago Press, 2015). I have drawn especially on Eudo C. Mason, 'Goethe's Sense of Evil', *Publications of the English Goethe Society*, 34 (1964), 1–53. In interpreting Goethe's self-definition in his letter to Lavater, I follow T. J. Reed, 'Goethe as Secular Icon', in John Walker (ed.), *The Present Word. Culture, Society and the Site of Literature: Essays in Honour of Nicholas Boyle* (London: Legenda, 2013), 44–51. On Goethe and Kant, I am indebted to Nicholas Boyle, 'Kantian and Other Elements in Goethe's "Vermächtniß"', *Modern Language Review*, 73 (1978), 532–49. On Goethe's affirmation of earthly life, see T. J. Reed, 'Der behauste Mensch: On being at Home in the Universe. Goethe, Kant, and Others', *Publications of the English Goethe Society*, 83 (2014), 137–48.

Index

E

F

G

H

T

U

V

W

Y